THE AMRIT

uncovered editions

Series editor: Tim Coates

Titles in the series

uncovered editions

THE AMRITSAR MASSACRE, 1919

GENERAL DYER IN THE PUNJAB

∞⋘⋙∞

London: The Stationery Office

First published 1920
© Crown Copyright

This abridged edition
© The Stationery Office 2000
Reprinted with permission.
All rights reserved. No part of this publication may be
reproduced, stored in a retrieval system, or transmitted in
any form or by any means – electronic, mechanical,
photocopying, recording or otherwise – without the prior
permission of the copyright owner. In the first instance write
to the Contracts and Rights Manager, The Stationery Office
Limited, St Crispins, Duke Street, Norwich NR3 1PD.

ISBN 0 11 702412 0

A CIP catalogue record for this book is available from the
British Library

Typeset by J&L Composition, Filey, North Yorkshire
Printed in the United Kingdom for The Stationery Office by
Biddles Limited, Guildford, Surrey.
TJ 869   C30   04/00

Uncovered Editions are historic official papers which have not previously been available in a popular form. The series has been created directly from the archive of The Stationery Office in London, and the books have been chosen for the quality of their story-telling. Some subjects are familiar, but others are less well known. Each is a moment of history.

Series editor: Tim Coates

Tim Coates studied at University College, Oxford and at the University of Stirling. After working in the theatre for a number of years, he took up bookselling and became managing director, firstly of Sherratt and Hughes bookshops, and then of Waterstone's. He is known for his support for foreign literature, particularly from the Czech Republic. The idea for "Uncovered Editions" came while searching through the bookshelves of his late father-in-law, Air Commodore Patrick Cave OBE. He is married to Bridget Cave, has two sons, and lives in London.

Mahatma Gandhi was the leader of the Indian Congress Party which sought independence for India by peaceful means.

At the time of the events described, India was under British rule. Indians had fought alongside the British in the First World War, and had made tremendous financial contributions to the British war effort.

The documents in this book detail what happened in Amritsar in the Punjab, northern India, in April 1919.

Both an army commission and a parliamentary commission investigated the events. In the following year, Brigadier-General Dyer made representations to Parliament about the way he had been treated by the army. His report is also included in this book.

India 1919

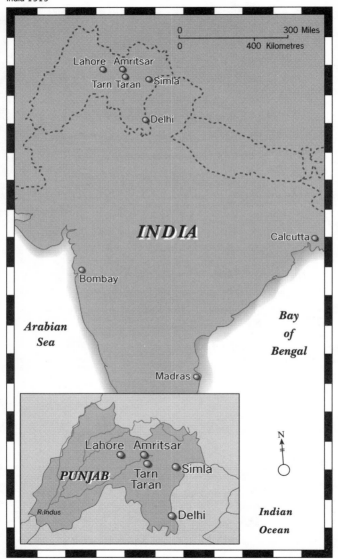

PART ONE

∞≪◊≫∞

Excerpts taken from the Report of the Hunter Committee appointed by the Government of India to investigate Disturbances in the Punjab, etc.
Cmd 681, 1920

THE MAJORITY REPORT

Circular issued by the secretary of the *Satyagraha Sabha* following Gandhi's arrest on 9th April 1919:

"The day before yesterday, *Mahatma* Gandhi started from Bombay for Delhi, Lahore, Amritsar, &c. On reaching Delhi yesterday night an order under the Defence of India Act was served on him requiring him not to go to Delhi, Punjab, and other places, and restricting him to Bombay. He disregarded the order; he is therefore arrested. He has expressed his desire that all residing in the *Ashram* will celebrate this day and will do their work with double zeal and faith. It is requested that the whole public will respect his desire."

Amritsar street plan

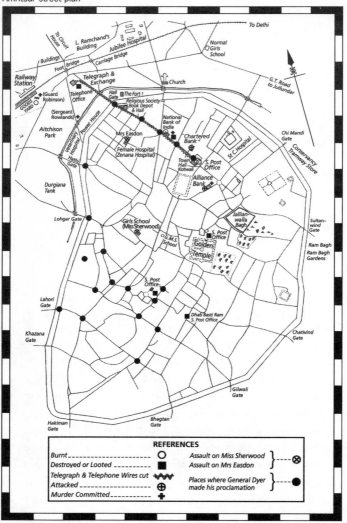

REFERENCES

Burnt	○	Assault on Miss Sherwood	⊗
Destroyed or Looted	■	Assault on Mrs Easdon	
Telegraph & Telephone Wires cut	〰		
Attacked	⊕	Places where General Dyer	●
Murder Committed	✛	made his proclamation	

∽∘⊲⊳∘∾

Amritsar District, April 1919

For some time before April 1919 public meetings about various questions, mostly but not entirely political, had shown that Amritsar had taken or was prepared to take great interest in public matters. It had been selected as the meeting place for the All-India Congress to be held in December 1919, and an All-India Congress Committee had been in existence since the end of 1917. The most active and influential "leaders"—certainly in the period just before the disturbance—were Drs. Kitchlew and Satyapal. Their speeches—some of which we have examined and some of which afterward came in question at their trial before a Tribunal established under martial law—show that on such points as the Rowlatt Bill, the expected Turkish Peace terms, and indeed on many, if not all, disputed matters, their attitude was one of very vigorous complaint against Government. In particular both of these gentlemen had joined Mr. Gandhi's civil disobedience movement and had taken the *Satyagraha* vow to disobey the Rowlatt Act and any other laws which a committee should select.

On the 23rd March a meeting was held in Amritsar in support of Mr. Gandhi's movement, and at another meeting on the 29th March a *Hartal*★ was decided on for the following day. On the 29th also Dr. Satyapal was served with an order, made by the Punjab Government under the Defence of India Act, prohibiting him from speaking in public. The *Hartal* on the 30th was successful beyond expectation and stopped the whole business of the city. There was no collision with the police and no resort to violence. On the 4th April Dr. Kitchlew was served with an order similar to that made against Dr. Satyapal.

Things were in this position when the question arose whether another *Hartal* should be held on the 6th, there having been some confusion at Amritsar, as at Delhi, as to the date which Mr. Gandhi had intended. In view of the troubles at Delhi on the 30th March the local Congress Committee seem to have declared against having another *Hartal*, and on the 5th the Deputy Commissioner was told by leading

★ A *Hartal* means a closing of shops and other businesses.

citizens that it would not take place. However, at a private meeting held in the late afternoon of the 5th, at which Dr. Kitchlew and Dr. Satyapal were present, a *Hartal* was decided on, and on the next day took full effect, business throughout Amritsar being once more stopped. This second time also the *Hartal* passed off peacefully and Europeans could and did walk unmolested amongst the crowds. A poster, however, was found exhibited at the Clock Tower calling on the people of Amritsar to "die and kill."

The Deputy Commissioner (Mr. Miles Irving) was much perturbed by the proof, afforded by the second *Hartal*, of the power and influence of Drs. Kitchlew and Satyapal. On the 8th April he addressed the Commissioner and the Punjab Government by letter upon this subject. Pointing out that from one cause or another the people were restless and discontented, he pressed urgently for an increase in the military forces, stating that with the existing garrison any resolute action in the city would leave the civil lines almost undefended. "As it is, we must abandon nine-tenths of the city to a riot, holding only the Kotwali and communications, and even so will be hard pressed to defend the station and civil lines." He viewed the *Hartal* as a mere step to test the organisation. "Who are at the bottom of this I cannot say. The Congress party are in the outer circle. They passed a resolution against a strike and promptly came to heel when Kitchlew ordered it. Kitchlew himself I regard as the local agent of very much bigger men. Who those are can only be guessed from their rage at the

Rowlatt Acts which strike at the roots of organised anarchic crime." The older type of leaders—Khan Bahadurs and Rai Sahibs—had in his opinion lost all influence. "I am trying to get into touch with the new leaders who have influence. I was wrong in thinking I could influence Kitchlew—he is too deep in. I may possibly get hold of some of the outer circle. But I have not much hope from them. I think that things will be worse before they are better and that for the present we must rely on ourselves alone."

The Punjab Government took prompt action upon this letter. As the orders of 29th March and 4th April showed, the conduct of Dr. Satyapal and Dr. Kitchlew had been under consideration. At an earlier stage the Deputy Commissioner had asked the Government to suspend action against Dr. Kitchlew in order that opportunity for persuasion might be given before resorting to any order, and, as already shown, the letter of 8th April refers to this fact. It does not appear that any actual breach of the orders against public speaking had been committed by either of the gentlemen. They had taken part in at least one private meeting and they had brought about the second *Hartal*, suddenly, with great completeness, and without warning to the authorities. The Punjab Government on the 9th April issued orders for their deportation from Amritsar and internment in Dharamsala, *i.e.*, in another district of the Punjab. This order was within the powers of the local Government under the Defence of India Act; sanction from the Imperial Government was not necessary and was not asked. The Deputy Commissioner's letter was passed on to the General Officer Commanding Division on the 9th with the statement "the Lieutenant-Governor agrees with Mr. Irving that the military garrison at Amritsar requires strengthening as early as possible."

The 9th April was the day of *Ram Naumi*—a Hindu festival on which cars are commonly drawn in procession accompanied by people raising cries in honour of Hindu deities. This practice was followed as usual in Amritsar, but, contrary to previous practice, the festival was, very largely, participated in by Muhammadans, and along with the usual shouts political cries were freely raised: "*Mahatma Gandhi ki jai*," "*Hindu-Mussalman ki jai*." The effect of the evidence before us is that the festival became a striking demonstration in furtherance of Hindu-Muhammadan unity—people of the different creeds drinking out of the same cups publicly and by way of a demonstration. To expect this form of unity to last beyond the day would doubtless be to expect too much; nor should it be condemned as wholly sinister or unreal because it did not last longer than mere demonstrations can. We think it clear that in Amritsar as elsewhere efforts towards "unity" had been made largely and indeed frankly in a political interest. That the disturbed state of political feeling in Amritsar would assist and did assist to throw the two warring creeds into a common camp *vis-à-vis* Government is intelligible enough. Dr. Kitchlew's influence in particular was, and had consistently been, in the direction of unity, and doubtless in Amritsar this fact accounts for more than does the general movement, which has for at least two years been well marked all over India. In these circumstances, while we regard the *Ram Naumi* festival in Amritsar as showing a state of considerable ferment, excitement, and unrest, and, as further proof of the influence of the local political leaders, we do not feel entitled to regard it as significant of special evil or to interpret the events which ensued after other causes had supervened by reading them in the light of a sinister construction of the facts of the 9th April. It is certain that the day passed off without any hostility being offered to Europeans. The Deputy Commissioner himself got caught in the crowd and witnessed a procession from the verandah of the Allahabad Bank. He says "as a rule they were very civil, every car in the procession stopped in front of me and the band played 'God Save the King.' A note of disloyalty which struck me was that a party of Muhammadan students dressed to represent the Turkish Army raised a rude demonstration by clapping their hands which is a sign of rudeness up here, that is all."

The orders of the local Government for the deportation of Drs. Kitchlew and Satyapal reached the Deputy Commissioner on the evening of the 9th. They were to be removed quietly to Dharamsala. In consultation with some other officials including Captain Massey, the Officer Commanding the station, the Deputy Commissioner decided to send for Dr. Kitchlew and Dr. Satyapal to come to his own house at 10 o'clock next morning and to have them

taken from there by motor car by the Superintendent
of Police (Mr. Rehill) and a small escort. Certain
arrangements to prevent a possible rescue were
decided on that night. In addition to these, other
arrangements were made in consultation with the
Officer Commanding (Captain Massey) for dealing
with any disorder which might ensue upon the
deportation becoming known. Apparently a labour
corps was in cantonments two miles away; from the
Amritsar garrison British Infantry were to be kept in
reserve at the Ram Bagh Gardens and mounted pickets were to be posted at the Rego bridge which leads
to the Fort, at the Hall Gate bridge, and at the
Hospital level-crossing. The police reserve—75 armed
men—were to be kept in the Kotwali. Certain other
police under a European officer, Mr. Marshall, were
to protect a level-crossing called the Police Lines
Crossing. It was further arranged that the Civil
Surgeon, Lieutenant-Colonel Henry Smith, I.M.S.,
should, in case of need, use his motor ambulance and
collect European women and children in the Fort.
Written orders were made by the Deputy
Commissioner, though not publicly promulgated, to
the effect that whereas he had reason to believe that
a mob from the city would attempt to approach the
District Court House with the intention of overawing by force or by show of criminal force the
constituted authorities, no body of persons exceeding
five would be allowed to pass the railway line. These
orders were given to three European magistrates, the
crossings were pointed out to them and they were

told to keep back any crowd, peacefully if possible, but by military force if necessary.

The arrangements above-mentioned were in substance the "internal defence scheme" for defending the civil station. They are sufficiently elaborate to suggest very grave apprehension in the Deputy Commissioner's mind as regards the consequences of carrying out the deportations. This is emphasised if we take into account the orders given next morning by Captain Massey to the officer at the Fort, to have his guns in position, to have a machine-gun ready to cover the women and children in case they stood in need of protection, not to hesitate to open fire if the mob made for the Fort or attacked the railway station, and so on. We think, however, that no one on the night of the 9th anticipated or had reason to anticipate that the next day would see disorders so grave as those which in fact took place. That a disorderly crowd of Dr. Kitchlew's and Dr. Satyapal's supporters might come to the civil station to try to overawe the Deputy Commissioner or at least to make a large and noisy demonstration; that this might lead to something worse, especially if large numbers were adrift in the civil lines beyond possibility of control—this is, we think, a fair measure of what, in the view of the Deputy Commissioner, had to be guarded against. The precautions as to evacuation of the women and children seem inconsistent with the absence of proper steps to warn Europeans not to go into the city as usual. But though it is a matter of great regret that such warning was not given, we do not think that it could or should have been anticipated that a murderous antipathy towards all Europeans would burst out as it did. The behaviour of the crowds upon 30th March and 6th April in no way indicated this and the presence of the whole reserve of armed police at the Kotwali must not be overlooked in this connection. As the Deputy Commissioner put the matter in his evidence before us:—"I reckoned up the possibility and provided for about three times as much but ten times would not have been enough." Precaution in some directions beyond the apparent necessities of the occasion does not entitle criticism after the event to exact more than reasonable precautions in other matters. In military preparations in particular thoroughness is not necessarily an index to the gravity of the occasion. In this case the arrangements made were but an application of a pre-arranged scheme of internal defence which had been previously thought out and had no special reference to the probabilities of the 10th.

In spite of the request contained in the Deputy Commissioner's letter of the day before that more troops should be sent to Amritsar, we think that he acted rightly in the circumstances in carrying out the deportation orders quickly and quietly and that he cannot reasonably be blamed for not refusing to do so until more troops were sent. He was not contemplating any "resolute action in the city"; he was contemplating disorder, but not on such a scale as occurred.

We think further that to keep a strong force of 75 armed police at the Kotwali and not to have these men scattered in isolated pickets throughout the city was a prudent and reasonable course. As it turned out, the scenes of the worst outrages were very close to the Kotwali and a strong striking force there could and should have been much more effective than isolated pickets. That it was almost wholly ineffective in the emergency which arose was in no way the fault of the Deputy Commissioner and could not have been foreseen by any one.

On the morning of the 10th, Drs. Kitchlew and Satyapal came about 10 a.m. to the Deputy Commissioner's house as requested. They were accompanied by some friends. In about half an hour they had left for Dharamsala by motor car as arranged. The friends were detained for about an hour so as to give the escort a start. There was no attempt at rescue.

10th April 1919 [*date of first outbreak of rioting*]

About 11.30, however, the news of the deportation was spreading in the city; shops were being closed on all sides and crowds were collecting. A large crowd formed in Hall Bazaar and made its way through Hall Gate and over Hall Bridge at the further side of which was a small picket of mounted troops. This crowd was excited and angry at the deportations and was undoubtedly making for the civil lines bent upon seeing the Deputy Commissioner. A Criminal Investigation Department Inspector, who gave evidence before us and whom we believe, stated that he was in the back portion of this crowd on the first slope of the road-bridge and that members of the crowd near him as they were going over the bridge and before they had been fired upon or turned back, were crying out, "where is the Deputy Commissioner? We will butcher him to pieces." Another witness, Dr. Muhammad Abdullah Fauq, stated that he was with this crowd and the cries were they must see the Deputy Commissioner, ask him where these leaders were, and if he would not grant their release, insist on themselves also being taken to the same place. It is an ascertained fact that this angry crowd, as it poured out of the city towards the bridge, took no notice of Europeans whom it met on the way. Mr. Jarman, the Municipal Engineer, passed it by and was not molested. There is on the evidence very slender ground for supposing that this crowd in its initial stages was possessed of, or by, any definite common intention save that of angry and obstreperous protest in force before the Deputy Commissioner at his house and for the purpose of overawing him. It was as events showed equal to anything but had not as yet resolved upon anything very definite. Violent and excited threats against the Deputy Commissioner we think there were, but it is not certain that these were many or that they were representative in the first phase of the disturbance. The mob had not armed themselves with sticks or *lathis*. Still it is abundantly clear that the crowd was no mere crowd of mourning, and that to represent it as a large but peaceful body bent on respectful, or even lawful, protest before authority is a travesty of facts. We consider that the

Deputy Commissioner was right, and had done no more than his duty, when he resolved to prevent entrance into the civil lines by any such crowd. Beyond this it remains undeniable of this particular crowd that it was likely to cause a disturbance of the public peace and that the public security was manifestly endangered by it.

This crowd was stopped by the mounted picket at the further end of the Hall Bridge. Mr. Beckett, an Assistant Commissioner, arrived soon afterwards to act as Magistrate on duty at that spot. The picket at this time consisted apparently of a non-commissioned officer armed with sword and revolver, four mounted British soldiers, two with lances and two with rifles, and three Indian sowars. They were on the ironwork at the top of the bridge facing the crowd some eight or ten yards off. Mr. Beckett did his best to make himself heard amid the shouts of the crowd and to explain that it would not be allowed to proceed. Three men in the front of the crowd seem to have endeavoured to persuade the rest to desist. In spite of them and of all that the Magistrate and the soldiers could do, the crowd pushed back the picket making the horses restive and uncontrollable by hitting them with sticks. The picket was pushed slowly back from the bridge and more quickly down the slope which leads from it to Madan's shop. Near this spot was a heap of half-bricks and stones and further crowds were already there. The crowd on both sides of the picket joined in stoning them. It is possible, but not proved, that at some stage before the stone throwing, one soldier fired in the air without orders. The Deputy Commissioner arrived on the spot as the stoning was going on, and endeavoured to rally the picket, but the horses would not stand up to or charge the crowd, so they were withdrawn about 100 yards to get them clear from the crowd and make a new stand. Mr. Beckett went to call reinforcements. Captain Massey, the Officer Commanding, passed on his way to the Ram Bagh from the railway station to bring up infantry. Before his arrival at the Ram Bagh another picket of mounted men, under Lieutenant Dickie, had left for the spot in support of the over-bridge picket. Infantry, under Lieutenant Brown, were marching for the station and Captain Massey gave instructions to use any conveyance that could be had to get to the station at once and to keep the crowd on the other side of the railway. Lieutenant Dickie's mounted party arrived first, took over the position and temporarily held up the crowd. By some misunder-standing of orders the original picket seems to have left the spot. The Deputy Commissioner left to go after Captain Massey and make arrangements for further help. Shortly afterwards Mr. Connor, an Assistant Commissioner, who had been detailed to proceed to the Kotwali, came upon Lieutenant Dickie's picket, he thinks some six or seven men, partly British and partly Indian—more probably four, two Indians and two British—trotting back at a fast pace and being badly stoned by a dense crowd. These missiles were stones for road-metalling, of which there was a collection some little way off, apparently on the other side of the rail-way line. Mr. Connor was asked by Lieutenant Dickie to send reinforcements. He halted and rallied the picket, told Lieutenant Dickie that he must not let the crowd into the civil lines, and that it was his duty to fire. On this two British soldiers of the picket dismounted, took cover behind some culverts and fired three or four shots each. Some of these took effect, three or four individuals being killed or wounded. The crowd was brought to a standstill at once; it may have retired somewhat, but did not disperse. In our opinion this resort to firing was completely justified as absolutely necessary in the circumstances and in no way exceeding the occasion.

Shortly afterwards, Mr. Plomer, Deputy Superintendent of Police, arrived from the police lines with 24 foot police and seven sowars. This was about 1 p.m. Two or three casualties were lying in front of Madan's shop. The police were marched towards the crowd and brought up with muskets loaded with buckshot at the "ready position" about 40 yards away. On this some local lawyers came forward and said they would take the crowd away. Mr. Plomer gave them a chance to do this, and they succeeded in taking the mob away from the foot-bridge and railway line in the direction of the Telegraph Office which is on the city side of the railway. This had been almost effected by the time Lieutenant Brown's party of infantry arrived followed a little later by further infantry. Both foot and road-bridges were taken over by the infantry and the police picket of 24 men took over the railway level crossing.

It is to be observed that by 1 o'clock the crowds making for the civil lines were not merely those who were attempting to approach *via* Hall Gate. Crowds were coming out also through Hathi Gate and Lohgar Gate. There was really one huge crowd stretching to Aitchison Park which had been one of the first places in which people had collected on that morning. Mr. Plomer estimates that 30,000 people were taking part in the total crowd. It is not possible to state with certainty the order in which acts and incidents occurred in different parts of the town; many of them appear to have taken place very quickly and at about the same time; some of them had been completed and others begun before the incident of the second firing which we will deal with next.

The foot-bridge and the road-bridge at Hall Gate having been cleared they were occupied each by a small infantry picket, a third picket being in reserve. In a short time the Deputy Commissioner had returned to this locality and was called first to the foot-bridge against which a hostile crowd was forming. This crowd withdrew on being threatened. Thereupon he was called to the road-bridge (Hall Bridge) as a large crowd had approached determined to rush the picket. He took some mounted men with him, and rode out in front of the picket endeavouring to get the crowd to disperse. Mr. Plomer did the same. Their efforts and warnings were persistent and repeated, but the crowd closed in and they had to fall back to the picket. Mr. Plomer rode forward again and told the crowd that firing would take place. Two Indian gentlemen were in front trying to assist by persuading the crowd to go back, and the Deputy Commissioner was reluctant to fire in case they might be hit. While he was still considering as to his orders, the crowd made a rush, at the same time stoning the picket. The non-commissioned officer in charge was given the necessary order, the crowd was fired upon and between 20 and 30 casualties ensued. This incident took place at about 2 p.m. At this stage, and of this crowd, we consider it certain that the temper and determination to violence was more obvious, more resolute, and more vicious than that which had been exhibited earlier in the day. We think that the order to fire was rightly given, and we can find no ground for saying that the necessity of the moment was in any way exceeded or abused.

Before the close of the incident just described great destruction had commenced in the city. Thus, when the Deputy Commissioner returned to the bridges near Hall Gate within half-an-hour of the first firing, he noticed that smoke was coming up from the National Bank. This was not later than 1.30 and probably not many minutes after 1 o'clock. Again, Mr. Plomer, who saw the attack upon the Telegraph Office, says that this was long before the second firing at Hall Bridge. Save for these facts, we propose to state the occurrences briefly without burdening our report by an attempt to arrive at the exact order of acts of destruction or to establish sequences upon which nothing turns.

∘∘⌯⌯∘∘

The Kotwali and the Town Hall of Amritsar stand facing each other on different sides of the road which runs (through a gateway joining the two buildings at one end) straight along to Hall Gate. A short distance from the gateway a street runs off to the right and a few yards down this street is the Chartered Bank. The side of this building is visible from the outside of the gateway across a grass plot enclosed by iron railings, and the building is from 50 to 80 yards from the Kotwali.

The National Bank is on the direct road from the Town Hall to Hall Gate. It is on the right-hand side of the road and about 238 yards from the Kotwali.

The Alliance Bank is a corner building about 198 yards from the Kotwali. As one comes from Hall Gate down Hall Bazaar, past the National Bank, and through the gateway above-mentioned, one has to pass between the Town Hall and the Kotwali for the whole length of these buildings, and, after turning somewhat to the right, one reaches the Alliance Bank.

At the National Bank, Mr. Stewart, the Manager, and Mr. Scott, the Assistant Manager, were brutally beaten to death by the mob; their bodies were burnt in a pile of bank furniture in the middle of the bank building and the building itself was sacked, set on fire, and completely gutted. The godowns at the rear, in which large quantities of piece goods were kept, were broken into and thrown open for looting.

The Alliance Bank was attacked; the Manager, Mr. G. M. Thomson, who attempted to defend himself with a revolver was cruelly murdered, and flung from the balcony on to the street; his body was burnt in the street under a pile of Bank furniture drenched in kerosene oil. The building itself was not destroyed. It is owned by Indians, and in view of the manifest race-hatred of the mob, we do not doubt that this fact made them spare it.

At the Chartered Bank, glass and other property had been smashed and some attempt made to set it on fire, when 25 armed constables from the Kotwali under Khan Sahib Ahmed Jan, Deputy Superintendent of Police, dispersed the crowd without any difficulty, simply rushing

at it and shouting "*pakro, pakro*,"* upon which the mob
ran away. This was not before 1.30 p. m., and may have
been later. The European Manager, Mr. J. W. Thomson,
and his Assistant, Mr. Ross, had taken refuge in an
upper storey; after some time—apparently about 3
o'clock—they were taken to the Kotwali, close at
hand, and the Deputy Superintendent of Police with
the bulk of his guard stayed on at the Chartered Bank
without further incident till about 5 p. m.

The Town Hall itself, and the sub-post office
attached to it, were set on fire under the nose of the
armed police reserve at the Kotwali. It seems that a
quantity of kerosene oil belonging to the Municipal
Committee was lying near or in the Town Hall, and
was used by the mob in setting fire to this and other
buildings such as the National Bank.

Before dealing with other outrages committed by
the mob, it is necessary to make special comment, as
regards those just mentioned, upon the inactivity of
the armed police reserve. This is necessary in fairness
to the Deputy Commissioner, whose arrangements
were broken down by the ineffective handling of this
reserve. On this morning, Khan Sahib Ahmed Jan,
Deputy Superintendent of Police (with 30 years'
service), assisted by Muhammad Ashraf Khan, City
Inspector of Police (25 years' service), was stationed
at the Kotwali in charge of the reserve, which consisted of 75 men with muskets and ammunition. Both
officers had long service and good records. In

* Seize! Seize!.

addition there were several other men belonging to the Kotwali and some 15 or 16 detectives, whose duty it was to go about the city and bring reports to the Kotwali. Khan Sahib Ahmed Jan had received Mr. Plomer's orders by the mouth of the City Inspector, and these were merely orders to take charge of the reserve. But he knew that trouble was apprehended, that Amritsar was in a condition of excitement, that he was there to maintain order with the force at his command, and that his 75 men were the police reserve for the whole city. The City Inspector was in the same position; any useful information that could be got it was their duty to obtain for themselves.

Unfortunately we find it difficult to accept as accurate the evidence of either officer on some important details and they conflict on material points. The Deputy Superintendent says that he kept his men in the rear of the Kotwali, as had been done on the 6th, to be out of sight of the crowds and not to excite them; and that this was the position until—at about 1.30 p.m.—he was called to aid at the Chartered Bank. The City Inspector's evidence is in conflict on this point. The Deputy Superintendent says that the crowds passed between the Kotwali and Town Hall through the gateway into Hall Bazaar until he left for the Chartered Bank. The City Inspector says this road and gate had been cleared and barred by a line of men since about noon. The Deputy Superintendent says that when he left for the Chartered Bank the fire in the Town Hall had not broken out. The City Inspector says that it had.

However the facts may be upon these matters, the police reserve was too late to save the Town Hall in front of them, much too late to save Mr. Thomson, of the Alliance Bank, and still more too late to save the National Bank, its officers or its property, from an attack that occupied the mob for hours. The godowns were being looted as late as 5 p.m. The Inspector-General of Police was of opinion after enquiry that in the case of the Chartered Bank, the Europeans were saved by the loyalty of their clerks who hid them so securely that the mob, having failed to find them, had practically left the building, when the Deputy Superintendent arrived with his guard, though a crowd was still in the street. The facts before us indicate the probability of this.

In any possible view both officers failed either to grasp, or to attempt to cope with, their responsibility. Their lack of initiative and of reasonable precaution and the direct consequences of this are too plain for argument. Seventy-five armed men resolutely handled could, with ordinary skill and alertness, have made impossible the outrages which took place close to the Kotwali.

It has not been proved before us that the attacks upon any of the banks were known at the Kotwali before the time at which aid was dispatched, but when the best is made of the story narrated by the two officers it is one of helplessness and muddle. There is no explanation of the burning of the Town Hall which stood in front of them save that it had a road at the back as well as in front. On this road highly excited crowds had been passing and the Inspector tells us that the police had had to threaten to fire on the crowd there in order to rescue Mr. Jarman, the Municipal Engineer. No steps whatever were taken to see what could be seen from the Kotwali or its immediate precincts, to get information about Hall Bazaar from the gateway, to keep an eye on the crowds at the back of the Town Hall, to keep a look-out in the direction of the Alliance Bank or any of the other banks which had been picketted on the *Hartal* of the 6th. The Deputy Superintendent did not even receive a single report from the detectives who were his only scouts. His conduct at the Chartered Bank was pointless and ineffective beyond excuse. He explains that when he got to the Chartered Bank he stayed there till 5 o'clock—up to 3 o'clock guarding the two Europeans, and thereafter when these had gone to the Kotwali to give the people an impression that the Europeans were still there so they would not assault the Kotwali. It is not clear upon his evidence that up to 1.30 he had done anything; it is clear that from that time until 5 o'clock he took no steps to make any enquiry or to do anything as regards the city or as regards his main reserve. He knew enough and more than enough to call for energetic action; the duty upon which he employed all his time and 25 of his armed men was idle and unnecessary after the first ten minutes; since the Europeans could have been brought at once to the Kotwali and a small picket left at the bank within easy hail of those headquarters.

When we have added to this narrative of the

police reserve that there were about a hundred unarmed constables scattered throughout Amritsar in the ordinary course, and that these did not come upon the stage in any part of the tragedy enacted in the city upon the 10th of April, we have done what we can to explain why the mobs were left uncontrolled and almost unchecked.

∘₀⊲◈⊳₀∘

When the crowd had been induced to withdraw from the foot and road-bridges after the first firing near Hall Gate, it retired towards the Telegraph Office. This office was shortly afterwards attacked from two sides, a mob from the Aitchison Park side joining in the destruction. Telephone instruments were smashed to pieces, and the Telephone Exchange with its switch-board and fittings destroyed. This put out of action the whole telephone system of the town. Captain Massey had previously on that morning ordered the Jemadar of the station guard to take a party to the foot-bridge so as to have the Telegraph Office under observation and be ready to go to its defence. This officer and his men managed to beat off the mob from the Telegraph Office, and to rescue Mr. Pinto, the Telegraph Master, as he was being seized and dragged from his room, but not without recourse to firing. Eighteen rounds were expended in this rescue and we have no difficulty in upholding this as entirely justified.

The goods yard was stormed, damaged and looted, and Guard Robinson of the North-Western Railway, who was going towards the foot-bridge in the course of his work was chased and brutally beaten to death. Mr. Bennett, the Station Superintendent, was caught and injured severely, but the station picket was in time to save his life. Telegraph wires were cut but the actual platform of the station was held by a picket and this portion of the station was not damaged.

Sergeant Rowlands, electrician to the Military Works, had gone into the city and was endeavouring to make his way back to the Fort when he was attacked near the Rego Bridge and murdered. His skull was battered in—apparently by a straining screw.

Miss Sherwood, a lady missionary, was pursued by a mob when bicycling in a narrow street in the city on her way to one of her schools. The assault has not been detailed to us by eye-witnesses, but it was investigated and described by a Martial Law Commission. Its brutality was well known at the time and is not in dispute: it need only be indicated here. She was intercepted and overtaken by the mob, knocked down by blows on the head and beaten while on the ground;

when she got up to run she was knocked down again more than once; a door which she tried to enter was slammed in her face; in the end she was left on the street because she was thought to be dead. We should not omit to point out that she was afterwards picked up by some Hindus by whose action she was enabled to receive medical attention in time, as we understand, to save her life.

Another incident, vividly showing that no European of either sex was safe from the mob is the search for Mrs. Easdon, the lady doctor in charge of the Zenana Hospital. This hospital was entered and twice ransacked to find her; she contrived to conceal herself on both occasions and the second search was discontinued before she had been discovered upon news reaching the rioters of loot at the National Bank.

The Indian Christian Church and the Religious Book Society's Depôt and Hall were burnt; an attempt to burn the Church Missionary Society's Girls' Normal School was frustrated by the police picket, from the police lines crossing, under Inspector Marshall.

Sub-post offices at the Golden Temple, Hajith Mandi and Dhal Basti Ram were looted. The first two as well as the office at the Town Hall were combined post and telegraph offices and at all three places the telegraph instruments and fittings were destroyed.

Looting—at least at the godowns of the National Bank—proceeded late into the evening; but almost all the acts of murder, arson, pillage and destruction which we have described took place in the early afternoon. Before nightfall, however, interruptions of communication were amounting to a serious attempt to isolate Amritsar. The Telegraph Office had been one of the first objectives of the mob, but the damage done before this mob was beaten off affected the telephone more than the telegraph system. Some telegraph wires had been cut at the goods yard, and by about 2 p.m. all railway telegraph wires near Amritsar were cut. During the day both telephone and telegraph wires were cut in many places throughout Amritsar and its environs. The railway police guard on the Calcutta mail fired on and scattered a party attempting to destroy the main line to Lahore. At Bhagtanwala railway station which is on the Tarn Taran line, and about one mile from the Golden Temple, the station building was looted and burnt in the afternoon; the goods-shed and a wagon were looted; the points-locks and the telegraph wires broken. At night Chheharta railway station was attacked by villagers who looted a goods train that was standing in the yard.

This narrative of mob violence, while doubtless not exhaustive, is sufficient to show the nature and character of the outbreak in all important respects. That it was anti-Government is clear at every stage; starting in anger at the action of Government in deporting the two local politicians it proceeded by attack upon post offices and the railway (which is really a State railway and is regarded as such). Almost, though not quite from the first, hostility to Government became a murderous antipathy to

Europeans—not merely to officials but to Europeans as such. The attack upon the banks was primarily motivated by this race-hatred which led and directed the desire for destruction and loot. The destruction of buildings associated with Christian institutions, or thought so to be, points firmly in the same direction. The records of the trials certainly go to show that the actual perpetrators of brutal murder were not representative of Amritsar citizens, but of what may be called the "hooligan" class, some of whom in Amritsar appear to have had a certain leadership or influence over those of their own kind. But the numbers of the crowds taking part in the general disturbance, the extent to which crime and destruction were carried out, the area which they covered, the time they lasted, the general political motive of defiance to authority and destruction of its emblems, instruments or agents are facts too clear to be gainsaid. We do not omit to notice and to signalise the fact that some Indian citizens were doing their best to reason with the crowds which had to be repulsed at Hall Bridge, that Miss Sherwood was ultimately taken care of by some Indians, and that Mrs. Easdon owed her life to her *chaprasi*.* Other efforts by sane and loyal citizens inside the city on that day we have no doubt there were. Of visitors to the Horse Fair, we know also that a stalwart band of Indian officers, sowars and daffardars were collected by Khan Bahadur Fazal Dad Khan, Rissaldar-Major of the 12th Cavalry, and

*Messenger, orderly.

volunteered their services to the officer at the Fort.

It is clear that the first brutalities were commenced at latest very early after the first firing at Hall Bridge, and it is possible that nothing, or nothing much, was done before this—that is, until the crowd saw that they would not get to the Deputy Commissioner's bungalow in the civil lines. The Criminal Investigation Department, Inspector Pandit Jiwan Lal, who saw the mob at the Telegraph Office says he heard shouts "They have killed our brethren and we will kill them," and that by this time they were armed with sticks. For this reason we have set out somewhat fully the facts as to this firing. That this act of a small and hard-pressed picket doing its duty at the latest moment possible, is in any degree a mitigating circumstance seems to us unreasonable. It angered some, and as an incitement it might well be effective with others. That it was the cause of the excesses on the 10th is merely untrue.

During the day European women and children were taken to the Fort, where they were retained in conditions of extreme discomfort. Lieutenant-Colonel Smith on the sound of the first firing went into the city with his ambulance and brought out some lady missionaries and Indian Christians. He returned to the Girls' School to find it being attacked by a mob which turned on him. He escaped with his ambulance and in the meantime the police picket at the Police Lines Crossing had gone to the rescue.

Between 1 and 2 o'clock a party of 1–9th Gurkhas, unarmed, but 260 strong, had arrived at the railway station on their way to Peshawar under Captain Crampton. These were detained. One hundred of them were armed from the Fort and pickets were strengthened. The railway station itself was now safe, and the Rego Bridge could be strongly guarded while the women and children were being got to the Fort.

Late that night—after 10 o'clock—300 troops— 125 British and 175 Baluchis—arrived from Lahore under Major Macdonald, who took over command from Captain Massey. Early on the 11th 300 more troops arrived from Jullunder—100 British and 200 Indian.

The Commissioner of the Division (Mr. A. J. W. Kitchen) aud the Deputy Inspector-General (Mr. D. Donald) arrived at the railway station from Lahore by motor car, at 5 o'clock on the evening of the 10th. A letter was brought from the Kotwali, stating that all the Europeans alive were inside that building and in no danger. It had been decided to send a party to fight its way into the city to rescue Europeans whose danger was obvious, but whose fate was unknown; on the letter being received this measure was postponed till the reinforcements should arrive from Lahore, as most of the Gurkhas were still without arms. Late at night, when Major Macdonald arrived with his men, the Commissioner told him verbally, that the situation was beyond civil control, and that he, as senior Military Officer, was to take such steps as the military situation demanded. He seems to have made it clear that these steps were to be for the purpose of re-establishing civil control. He further asked that a party be sent into the city to get information and bring out the surviving Europeans. This party was dispatched. Mr. Plomer, the Deputy Superintendent of Police, went with the party, but no civil magistrate was sent, as it was thought to be a purely military operation in which the presence of a civil magistrate would embarrass the military officer. Instead of the party having to fight its way through the streets, as the Commissioner anticipated, the streets were found deserted. The Chartered Bank officers—Messrs. Thomson and Ross—together with Mr. Jarman and a Sergeant Parsonage, who had taken refuge in the Kotwali, were brought out in safety.

11th April 1919

The total number of persons killed on the 10th by the fire of the troops was approximately 10; the number wounded must be greater. On the 11th certain persons from the city came to the civil lines to arrange as to processions for the burying of the dead. The Commissioner says they appeared to him to be representing the rioters and that their attitude was defiant. There had been an intention of holding these burials in the Jallianwala Bagh, and again of holding large processions to the usual burial place outside the city. In the end these emissaries were told that only small parties would be allowed to go to the burial ground;

that the funerals must be commenced at 2 o'clock
and that by 4 the parties must be back in the city.
These orders were not agreed to, but in fact they were
ultimately carried out—the dead were taken from
Khair-ud-din's Mosque out by the Sultanwind Gate;
large processions both of Hindus and Muhammadans
seem to have followed in the city but not further. A
witness speaks to rumours being circulated among
the crowd at the mosque, that at Lahore the Fort and
Anarkali had been occupied by Indian troops who
had rebelled. This rumour was in existence the previous day as the Commissioner himself heard of it on
the 10th.

The persons who came to arrange as to the
funerals were mostly young lawyers. A notice signed
by the Deputy Commissioner was handed to them
that they might distribute and explain it to the people
in the city. This was at that time thought to be the
only practicable method of publication. The notice
stated, "The troops have orders to restore order in
Amritsar and to use all force necessary. No gatherings
of persons nor processions of any sort will be allowed.
All gatherings will be fired on. Any persons leaving
the city in groups of more than four will be fired on.
Respectable persons should keep indoors." The
Principal of the Khalsa College was also asked to get
his students to tell the people that the authorities
considered that a state of war had broken out and
they must settle down. All third class booking to
Amritsar by rail was stopped as the Baisakhi festival
was approaching and it was desired to prevent inno-

cent strangers from coming into so grave a situation.

A party of a hundred rifles went into the city as far as the Kotwali leaving strong pickets at the side streets.

From this time the Kotwali and its approaches were held by troops. A Magistrate was sent to Tarn Taran to do what he could there by local levies as no troops could be spared from Amritsar. The Tahsildar at Ajnala was given similar instructions. Orders were given to village headmen to get villagers to keep watch and ward on the railway line. No business was going on in Amritsar and much time seems to have been spent upon the question of the funerals.

On the evening of the 11th the Commissioner left for Lahore, and later Brigadier-General R. E. H. Dyer, C.B., who commanded the Jullunder Brigade, arrived at Amritsar and took over charge from Major Macdonald. He transferred headquarters from the railway station to the Ram Bagh.

∘₀⟨∢⟩₀∘

12th April 1919

On the 12th a strong column under General Dyer marched round the city as crowds were reported to be collecting outside it. These were made to go back peaceably and the troops went into the city to the Kotwali. Small parties of troops were sent with police to make arrests in connection with the crimes of the 10th and several important arrests were made. General Dyer says that the bearing of the inhabitants was most insolent and many spat on the ground as the troops passed. At one point—the Sultanwind Gate—there were shouts of "Hindu-Mussalman *ki jai*," and the mob was dispersed with difficulty. The advisability of opening fire was considered by the General, but he refrained, as he thought he should first warn the people by a proclamation. Accordingly on this day a proclamation was drawn up in the following terms: —

> "The inhabitants of Amritsar are hereby warned that if they will cause damage to any property or will commit any acts of violence in the environs of Amritsar it will be taken for granted that such acts are due to incitement in Amritsar city, and offenders will be punished according to Military Law.
>
> "All meetings and gatherings are hereby prohibited, and will be dispersed at once under Military Law."

The issue of this proclamation, which was formally signed by the Brigade-Major on General Dyer's behalf, was left to the police; it does not appear what steps were taken to ensure its publication.

On the 12th also a small force was sent from Amritsar to Tarn Taran. By some misunderstanding this force was brought back at night instead of remaining there as intended. On its leaving a large crowd of villagers assembled to loot the *tahsil*, but the Inspector of Police turned out with a small body of men, and, by showing a bold front, drove off the crowd. Troops were sent there on the next day and stayed there.

During the day telegraph wires were cut between Chheharta and Amritsar, between Khasa and Gurusar, and between Khasa and Chheharta. About midnight the railway line was torn up between Chheharta and Khasa and a goods train was derailed.

13th April 1919 [*day of the massacre in Amritsar*]

On the morning of the 13th April General Dyer went through the city in company with the District Magistrate and some others and had a proclamation read out by the *naibtahsildar* to the people, who were summoned by beat of drum at a considerable number of different places. From an examination of the map, showing the different places where the proclamation was read, it is evident that in many parts of the city the proclamation was not read. The proclamation, as drawn up in English, is in these terms:

"It is hereby proclaimed, to all whom it may concern, that no person residing in the city is

permitted or allowed to leave the city in his own
or hired conveyance, or on foot without a pass.
No person residing in the Amritsar city is permitted to leave his house after 8. Any persons
found in the streets after 8 are liable to be shot.
No procession of any kind is permitted to parade
the streets in the city, or any part of the city, or
outside of it, at any time. Any such processions or
any gathering of four men would be looked upon
and treated as an unlawful assembly and dispersed
by force of arms if necessary."

It is said that many people, on hearing this proclamation read, did not treat it seriously, but that remarks
were made that it was bluff, that the General would not
fire, and not to be afraid. At the time when General
Dyer's proclamation was being read out a counter-
proclamation was made to the effect that a meeting
would be held in the afternoon in the Jallianwala
Bagh. A meeting had been held on the 12th April
in the compound of the Hindu Sabha School, at which
an announcement had been made for a meeting to be
held at the Jallianwala Bagh on the 13th April.

About 1 o'clock General Dyer heard that the
people intended to hold a big meeting about 4.30
p.m. On being asked why he did not take measures to
prevent its being held, he replied, "I went there as
soon as I could. I had to think the matter out; I had
to organise my forces and make up my mind as to
where I might put my pickets. I thought I had done
enough to make the crowd not meet. If they were
going to meet I had to consider the military situation

and make up my mind what to do, which took me a certain amount of time."

It may be noted that in consequence of information received from neighbouring villages detachments of troops had been sent to various places.

About 4 o'clock in the afternoon of 13th April General Dyer received definite information that a meeting was being held at Jallianwala Bagh contrary to the terms of the proclamation issued by him that morning. He then proceeded through the city with a number of pickets, which he left at pre-arranged places, and a special force of 25 Gurkhas and 25 Baluchis armed with rifles, 40 Gurkhas armed only with kukris, and two armoured cars. On arriving at Jallianwala Bagh he entered with this force by a narrow entrance which was not sufficiently wide to allow the cars to pass. They were accordingly left in the street outside.

The Jallianwala Bagh is not in any sense a garden as its name would suggest. It is a rectangular piece of unused ground, covered to some extent by building material and *débris*. It is almost entirely surrounded by the walls of buildings. The entrances and exits to it are few and imperfect. It seems to be frequently used to accommodate large gatherings of people. At that end of the Bagh by which General Dyer entered there is raised ground on each side of the entrance. A large crowd had gathered at the opposite end of the Bagh and were being addressed by a man on a raised platform about 100 yards from where General Dyer stationed his troops. According to the report sent by

General Dyer to the Adjutant-General after the occurrence the crowd numbered about 6,000. It is probable that it was much more numerous, and that from 10 to 20,000 people were assembled.

As soon as General Dyer entered the Bagh he stationed 25 troops on one side of the higher ground at the entrance and 25 troops on the other side. Without giving the crowd any warning to disperse, which he considered unnecessary as they were in breach of his proclamation, he ordered his troops to fire and the firing was continued for about 10 minutes. There is no evidence as to the nature of the address to which the audience was listening. None of them were provided with firearms, although some of them may have been carrying sticks.

As soon as firing commenced the crowd began to disperse. In all 1,650 rounds were fired by the troops. The firing was individual and not volley firing. Many casualties occurred among the crowd. As General Dyer, when the firing ceased, immediately marched his troops back to the Ram Bagh just outside the city, there was no means at the time of forming a correct estimate of the number killed and wounded. At first it was thought that about 200 had been killed, and this number was apparently referred to as the list of casualties. Recently an investigation into the numbers has been completed by the Government with the assistance of a list compiled by the Allahabad *Seva Samiti*.★ As a result of this investigation it was

★Social service league

discovered that approximately 379 people were killed. Of these about 87 were strangers or villagers who had come into Amritsar from the neighbouring district. No figure was given for the wounded, but their number may be taken as probably three times as great as the number of killed.

After the firing at Jallianwala Bagh no serious outbreak occurred in Amritsar. Shops continued to be shut for some days, but the life of the city gradually resumed a more normal aspect. In the immediate vicinity there was an attempted dacoity by the villagers of Ballarwal on that of Makhowal and one or two cases of wire-cutting, but otherwise there was nothing further calling for notice in this area.

✺

Sir Michael O'Dwyer's approval

The first communication that reached Lahore of what had occurred at Jallianwala Bagh was in a mutilated message to the Deputy Inspector-General of the Criminal Investigation Department at about 11 or 11.15 on the night of the 13th. It was telephoned to Mr. Thompson, the Chief Secretary, in the following terms:—

> "11.30 p. m. Got message from the Deputy Commissioner, Amritsar, much mutilated. Sense seems to be—seven arrests were made to day and a prohibited meeting dispersed. Communicated to Colonel Gasnell who had no

report from the General Officer Commanding
Amritsar. Rumours heavy casualties in Amritsar
to-day."

About 3 a.m. on the 14th two gentlemen arrived by
motor-car with a communication from the District
Magistrate. The Lieutenant-Governor was informed
of this message. It was to the effect that the meeting
at Jallianwala Bagh had been dispersed by force and
that the death casualties amounted to about 200. Sir
Michael O'Dwyer says that he was informed at the
time. He asked for details from General Beynon. Early
next morning General Beynon telephoned General
Dyer's report to the Lieutenant-Governor's Private
Secretary. "I made no record of the message," says Sir
Michael O'Dwyer. "It showed as far as I can remember that General Dyer had used only Indian and
Gurkha troops, that he was accompanied by the
Superintendent of Police. I am stating the message as
I remember to have received it—that he had to disperse a mob of several thousands assembled in open
defiance of his proclamation that morning, that the
dead casualties had been about 200 and that order had
been completely restored in Amritsar. That was the
message briefly as far as I remember it. It was General
Beynon's summary of the message he had received
from General Dyer, and General Beynon, who is
General Dyer's superior, said that he fully approved of
General Dyer's action and asked if he might convey
my approval." According to Sir Michael the time was
not one for disputing the necessity of military action.

"I approved of General Dyer's action in dispersing by force the rebellious gathering and thus preventing further rebellious acts. It was not for me to say that he had gone too far when I was told by his superior officer that he fully approved General Dyer's action. Speaking with perhaps a more intimate knowledge of the then situation than anyone else, I have no hesitation in saying that General Dyer's action that day was the decisive factor in crushing the rebellion, the seriousness of which is only now being generally realised."

∞◦◅❂▻◦∞

Martial law was declared in Amritsar on 15th April.

Some of the orders issued [in connection with the martial law] were injudicious. They served no good purpose and were not drawn with sufficient tact to prevent undue annoyance to the civil population.

The most criticised of these orders is, probably, what has come to be known as General Dyer's crawling order.

On 10th April Miss Sherwood, while bicycling in Amritsar, had been brutally assaulted and left for dead in a street of the city. The perpetrators of this dastardly offence were deserving of the severest punishment. Some days after the assault had been committed General Dyer erected a triangle or whipping post at the place where Miss Sherwood fell. His intention was that those who had been guilty of the assault should be publicly flogged at this triangle. He placed two pickets at different parts of the street with instructions that no Indians were to pass between these points of the street, but he added that if they had to pass they must go on all-fours. This order was issued on the 19th April, *i.e.*, 9 days after the assault had been committed on Miss Sherwood. It continued in force until 26th April, when it was withdrawn on the instructions of the Punjab Government, who disapproved of it.

At the time when he issued the order General Dyer says that it never entered his brain that any sensible or sane man would intentionally go through the street, which he desired to close. Unfortunately, just after he gave the order to the picket, some men were brought by the police before General Dyer for not salaaming and, on account of their impertinent demeanour to him, he ordered them to be arrested and taken to the police office. These men were taken by the police past the picket, who insisted on their crawling. General Dyer, however, explains that, in ordering their arrest and removal to the jail, he had no idea that they would pass along the street to which the crawling order applied. On the following day six men were sentenced to be flogged for some breach of fort discipline—the exact nature of their offence was not proved. They appear to have been under arrest for the assault on Miss Sherwood. They were taken to the whipping post and there flogged. On their way from the picket to the post and back they were made to crawl. We understand that these six men were afterwards convicted of the offence against Miss Sherwood with which they were charged. In addition to the cases we have mentioned other people had to crawl along the street. Altogether about 50 people seem to have done so. There are a number of houses that abut on the street. The inhabitants of these houses have occasion to use the street for the purpose of getting the necessaries of life or on other legitimate occasion. General Dyer thought all the houses had back entrances, but in this he was wrong. On this error being pointed out to him he suggested that it was only a slight inconvenience for the people to go on the roofs of the houses and improvise other means of getting supplies than using the street. In this we cannot agree. The order is certainly open to the objection that it caused unnecessary inconvenience to a number of people, and that it unnecessarily punished innocent as well as guilty. Above all, from an administrative point of view, in subjecting the Indian population to an act of humiliation, it has continued to be a cause of bitterness and racial ill-feeling long after it was recalled.

∞◦◌◦∞

THE MINORITY REPORT

Circumstances existing at the beginning of 1919.

In order to arrive at a correct conclusion regarding the real nature of the disorders of April 1919, it is necessary to bear in mind the circumstances existing in the beginning of the year 1919, in the country generally and in the places where these disorders broke out in particular.

For four years and more the resources of India, like those of the other members of the British Empire, had been strained to the utmost in the prosecution of the war. A large effective army had been supplied, the Punjab itself making a substantial contribution of 400,000. India has raised three war loans, and contributed 100,000,000 *l.* as its quota to the Empire's War expenses. Besides the direct contributions in men and money there were indirect contributions of a substantial character in various ways. The prices of necessaries of life and other commodities of daily use had increased immensely owing to the war, pressing very heavily on the middle classes and people of limited means. People with fixed moderate incomes were most hard-hit in this direction, and among them were the subordinate Railway officials, who were, therefore, discontented. Curtailment of facilities of travelling and of import and export of merchandise had also created considerable hardship. The operations of the Defence of India Act and the rules thereunder, and of the Press Act, had encroached upon the ordinary standard of liberty.

While the war was on, all the restraints and hardships, though felt bitterly, were suffered patiently, because of the common purpose of winning the war. But the people generally had hoped that the defeat of Germany and the successful ending of the war for the Allies would immediately end the abnormal conditions and bring into existence a happy and prosperous era. After the Armistice was concluded in November 1918, the prevailing abnormal conditions, instead of vanishing, became aggravated, particularly in relation to high prices. The ordinary people naturally became discontented with their lot. There was widespread famine in the country owing to the failure of the monsoon of 1918, and the prevalence of influenza and other epidemics had resulted in a very heavy mortality. The new Income Tax Act and the more searching methods of inquiry in relation thereto, as well as the interference with trade conditions already referred to, had made the trading community restless.

The War had also created throughout the world a new outlook of freedom and liberty, and the same had visibly affected India. The Imperial Government had, as early as August 1917, made a declaration of policy by which the attainment by India of Responsible Government by successive stages was put forward as the goal and the Secretary of State for India and the Viceroy, having gone round the country and ascertained the views of the public as to the manner in which that policy was to be given effect to, had published the Montagu-Chelmsford Scheme. Great expectations were thereby raised, and when it was said that the Government of India were likely to suggest modifications therein of a somewhat illiberal character, that news had caused considerable irritation. The conclusion of the war has also brought forward the thorny question of the terms on which peace was to be concluded with Turkey; and the Muhammadans in India were apprehensive that those terms would be severe.

The above statement describes the factors that were influencing the minds of the people throughout the country, including the Punjab and the other places where these disorders took place.

Some of the above factors were more potent in the Punjab than elsewhere. As already observed, the Punjab had supplied by far the largest number of combatants as compared to the other provinces in India, and it is quite natural that owing to casualties amongst them, war-weariness would be more pronounced in the Punjab than in any other province. Similarly, the restrictions on traffic must have been more seriously felt by the producer of the Punjab which every year exports a large quantity of food-stuffs. Lahore, Amritsar, Gujranwala, Wazirabad, Hafizabad, Sangla, Chuharkana, Alkalgarh, Aminabad, Kasur, Patti, Khem Karan, came under the special income tax and the increase was very large, ranging from 100 to 200 per cent. The seizure of wheat stocks under the Defence of India Act to stop speculation and reduce the price of grain to the poor was also naturally disliked by the traders affected thereby. Then the Punjab Government under Sir Michael O'Dwyer had for various reasons come to be regarded by the educated and politically minded classes as opposed to their aspirations. His speech in the Imperial Legislative Council in September 1917, was regarded as an attack on the educated classes and created considerable resentment. At the next meeting he expressed regret that his speech had hurt people's feelings. During his administration orders had been issued prohibiting politicians like Mrs. Besant and Mr. Tilak from entering the Punjab and reports of the proceedings of certain meetings had been prohibited publication unless they had been censored. He had objected to the Hon'ble Dr. Sapru, the Hon'ble Mr. Bannerji and the Hon'ble Pandit Madan Mohan Malavya being invited to attend the Conference that was held at Lahore to support the reforms-proposals of the nineteen members of the Indian Legislative Council. Several newspapers had been prohibited entry into the Punjab; and the Press Act had been put into operation more vigorously there than in any other province. The Hon'ble Mr. Thompson, Chief Secretary to the Punjab Government, said that the late Lieutenant-Governor of the Punjab wanted the atmosphere of the place to be as calm as possible during the war, and that all these measures taken by him in regard to the Press and Political agitation must be regarded as war-measures. In referring to these measures, we must not be regarded as attempting in any manner to pronounce judgment as to their merits; we are referring to them only with the object of noting the fact that in consequence of them there was considerable feeling existing in the minds of the educated and thinking classes in the Punjab.

On the 18th January 1919, what are popularly known as the Rowlatt Bills were published and were introduced in the Imperial Legislative Council on the 6th February 1919. The bills evoked almost universal opposition in the country. They were opposed by almost all the Indian members of the Imperial

Legislative Council, of all shades of political opinion
in the country. It was felt in India that, when she
stood steadfastly by the Empire in the War and had
thereby proved her right to be treated as an equal
member of the Empire, repressive legislation of this
character was being hurriedly passed while the
Reforms Scheme for instalment of Self-Government
had not till then materialised. But the main objection
to the legislation was that the Executive were being
clothed thereby with considerable powers uncontrolled by the judiciary. When an amendment moved
by the Hon'ble Mr. Surendra Nath Bannerji for the
postponement of the bill to the September session,
pointing out that there was no harm in so doing, as
the Defence of India Act was still in operation, was
negatived, considerable feeling of resentment was created. In stating the above facts we must not be
regarded as in any manner expressing any opinion on
the question whether the introduction of these measures at this juncture was unwise or with regard to the
merits of those measures; it will be outside the scope
of our reference to do so. We have stated these circumstances only with the object of taking note of the
fact that the introduction of the Rowlatt Bills did create considerable resentment throughout the country.
This opposition, shared in as it was by people of all
shades of political opinion, was genuine and not a fac-
tious or artificial one as was suggested by some
witnesses before us. One of the Rowlatt Bills was
finally passed in the Legislative Council on the 17th
March 1919, and received the assent of the Viceroy

soon afterwards. The agitation against the measure increased, and demonstrations of various kinds were made to secure the repeal of the measure. It appears that at any rate in the Punjab there were afloat a considerable number of misrepresentations of the provisions of the Rowlatt Act, but it was not suggested that any known or recognised leaders were responsible for these misrepresentations. Although these misrepresentations were current for a considerable time Government had not taken any definite step to explain the Act to people at large; it was not until after the *Hartal* of April 6th that the Punjab Publicity Board took steps to distribute copies of it in large numbers.

The firing at the Jallianwala Bagh.

What the military authorities did at Amritsar up to the declaration of martial law is, as has already been observed, taken by the Punjab Government as done in the aid of the civil authority, and they say that such action will be governed by sections 130–131 of the Criminal Procedure Code. The action of the civil authorities, in asking the Officer Commanding "to consider himself in charge of the military situation and to take such steps as he thought necessary to re-establish civil control," it may be argued, amounted to the establishment of *de facto* martial law, but for the purposes of judging the Jallianwala Bagh incident, it is immaterial whether General Dyer was acting merely in aid of the civil powers or on his own initiative as the Military Commander at a place where *de facto* martial law existed. On the morning of the 13th of April, General Dyer issued a proclamation, the relevant portion of which order for this purpose is as follows: —

> "No procession of any kind is permitted to parade the streets in the city or any part of the city or outside it at any time. Any such processions or gatherings of four men will be looked upon as unlawful assembly, and will be dispersed by force of arms if necessary."

It appears that this proclamation was promulgated by General Dyer himself, who went to certain parts of the town with the *Naib-tahsildar* and others. The people were collected at certain places by beat of drum and the proclamation was made known to them in the vernacular; printed copies of the Urdu translation of the proclamation were also distributed. There was produced before us a map of the city with the route followed by General Dyer, and the places at which the proclamation was promulgated marked on the map. There is no doubt, on this map and other evidence placed before us, that the proclamation was insufficiently promulgated, important portions of the town having been left out. The number of people who could have heard the proclamation promulgated

is put down at 8 to 10,000 people; the total population of the city is put down at 160,000 to 170,000.
There was a large influx of people from outside
owing to the *Baisakhi* fair which is an important religious festival; and there was also a cattle fair. The
reason for this insufficient promulgation is given in
the evidence of Mr. Plomer, Deputy Superintendent
of Police:—

> Q. You thought that was sufficient notice for a
> town like Amritsar to give of an important
> proclamation?
> A. I did not think anything. When it was too
> hot to walk in the city I took the nearest route
> out.
> Q. You did not suggest to the General that a
> longer time might be given?
> A. No. When we got to the Majid *mandir* the
> General remarked that it was getting too hot for
> the troops so I took the route to Lohgar Gate.
> Q. And then this proclamation was stopped?
> A. Yes.

No attempt was made to put up printed copies of
the proclamation at the entrance of the Jallianwala
Bagh, although it is said, as will be seen hereafter, that
it was the place where a number of public meetings
had previously been held. General Dyer returned to
his camp at Ram Bagh at 12.40 p. m., and on his
arrival there he learnt that a big meeting was going to
be held at Jallianwala Bagh at 4.30 p. m. It appears
that General Dyer, as soon as he heard about the

contemplated meeting, made up his mind to go there with troops and fire. He intended to fire upon them with machine guns, but he was unable to use machine guns owing to the accident of his being unable to take the armoured cars into the narrow entrance leading to the Bagh. When he took the machine guns with him he did not know of this difficulty as he had never seen the place before. Similarly, if he had more troops available than the 50 he had, according to him, he would have ordered all of them to fire. When he reached there, he saw a large meeting of people squatting on the ground and being addressed by a person from a small platform. The number of those attending the meeting are varyingly estimated from 15,000 to 20,000, but General Dyer at the time believed it to be 5,000 or 6,000. He put 25 Baluchis and 25 Ghurkhas on the raised ground at the entrance, and without giving any warning or asking the people to disperse, immediately opened fire at the people in the meeting, who were at a distance of 100 to 150 yards. The people, as soon as the first shots were fired, began to run away through the few exits the place has got, but General Dyer continued firing till the ammunition ran short. In all 1,650 rounds were fired, and the casualties have now been ascertained to be at least 379 killed and about 1,200 wounded.

His was not the case of a person who had to take a quick decision on a sudden emergency. After he received the information about the contemplated meeting he had four hours to think before he started to go to Jallianwala; he took half-an-hour to reach there, and he arrived there with his mind already made up as to the action he was going to take. His action was in accordance with a determined resolution that he had deliberately arrived at.

In the report he made on the 25th August, 1919, to the General Staff, 16th Division, General Dyer says:

"I fired and continued to fire till the crowd dispersed, and I considered that this is the least amount of firing which would produce the necessary moral and widespread effect it was my duty to produce if I was to justify my action. If more troops had been at hand the casualties would have been greater in proportion. *It was no longer a question of merely dispersing the crowd*, but one of producing a sufficient moral effect, from a military point of view, not only on those who were present, but more specially throughout the Punjab. There could be no question of undue severity."

Then in the evidence before us, General Dyer said:—

Q. I think you had an opportunity to make up your mind while you were marching to decide what was the right course. You came to the conclusion that if there really was a meeting, the right thing for you would be to fire upon them straightaway?

A. I had made up my mind. I was only wondering whether I should do it or I should not.

Q. No question of having your forces attacked entered into your consideration at all?

A. No. The situation was very, very serious. I had made up my mind that I would do all men to death if they were going to continue the meeting.

Q. Does it or does it not come to this; you thought that some striking act would be desirable to make people not only in Amritsar but elsewhere to consider their position more correctly?

A. Yes. I had to do something very strong.

Q. You commenced firing the moment you had got your men in position?

A. Yes.

Q. The crowd had begun to go away when you continued firing?

A. Yes.

Q. The crowd were making an effort to go away by some of the entrances at the further end of the Bagh?

A. Yes.

Q. You put your pickets one to the right and one to the left of the entrance. Towards some places the crowd was getting thicker than other places?

A. They did.

Q. From time to time you changed your firing and directed it to places where the crowds were thickest?

A. That is so.

Q. Is that so?

A. Yes.

Q. And for the reasons you have explained to us

you had made up your mind to open fire at the crowd for having assembled at all?

A. Quite right.

Q. When you heard of the contemplated meeting at 12.40 you made up your mind that if the meeting was going to be held you would go and fire?

A. When I heard that they were coming and collecting I did not at first believe that they were coming, but if they were coming to defy my authority and really to meet after all I had done that morning, I had made up my mind that I would fire immediately in order to save the military situation. The time had come now when we should delay no longer. If I had delayed any longer I was liable for court-martial.

Q. Supposing the passage was sufficient to allow the armoured cars to go in, would you have opened fire with the machine guns?

A. I think, probably, yes.

Q. In that case the casualties would have been very much higher?

A. Yes.

Q. And you did not open fire with the machine guns simply by the accident of the armoured cars not being able to get in?

A. I have answered you. I have said if they had been there the probability is that I would have opened fire with them.

Q. With the machine-guns straight?

A. With the machine-guns.

Q. I gather generally from what you put in your report that your idea in taking this action was really to strike terror? That is what you say. It was no longer a question of dispersing the crowd, but one of producing a sufficient moral effect.

A. If they disobeyed my orders it showed that there was complete defiance of law, that there was something much more serious behind it than I imagined, that therefore these were rebels, and I must not treat them with gloves on. They had come to fight if they defied me, and I was going to give them a lesson.

Q. I take it that your idea in taking that action was to strike terror?

A. Call it what you like. I was going to punish them. My idea from the military point of view was to make a wide impression.

Q. To strike terror not only in the city of Amritsar, but throughout the Punjab?

A. Yes, throughout the Punjab. I wanted to reduce their *morale*; the *morale* of the rebels.

Q. Did you observe that after the firing was opened, there were a number of people who lay on the ground in order to save themselves?

A. Yes.

Q. And your men continued to fire on these people who were lying on the ground?

A. I cannot say that. I think that some were running at the time, and I directed them to fire, and sometimes I stopped firing and re-directed

the firing on other targets. The firing was
controlled.

Q. Did you direct the firing on people who
were lying down in order to save themselves?

A. I probably selected another target. There
might have been firing on the people who were
still lying down, though I think there were
better targets than that.

This extract supplies the key to the action of
General Dyer. He fired on this meeting, and killed
about 400 people and wounded about 1,200; because,
in his view, they were rebels and he was "going to
give them a lesson," and "punish them," and "make a
wide impression," and "strike terror throughout the
Punjab," and he "wanted to reduce the *morale* of the
rebels." That was why he began to fire without warning and without calling upon them to disperse. He
continued firing even when the people began to run
away, and went on firing till his ammunition was
nearly exhausted.

Now because certain people, on the 10th April,
had committed certain outrages at Amritsar, to treat
the whole population of Amritsar as rebels was unjustifiable; it was still more unjustifiable to fire at the
meeting which was not engaged in doing any
violence, in order to give them a lesson and to punish them, because they had disobeyed his orders
prohibiting meetings. It is clear that there must have
been a considerable number of people who were perfectly innocent and who had never in all probability

heard of the proclamation. The Punjab Government
in their case submitted to us say that large crowds of
villagers had collected for the *Baisakhi* fair; and that
"there were a considerable number of peasants present at the Jallianwala Bagh meeting on the 13th; but
they were there for other than political reasons." And
they say in another part, "It is clear that a considerable
number of them (villagers) did attend as spectators."
It is therefore obvious that the crowd on which
General Dyer fired comprised people who did not
belong to the city of Amritsar at all, and who, therefore, cannot even vicariously be held responsible for
the acts of the hooligans on the 10th April. General
Dyer said in his evidence as follows: —

> Q. On the assumption that there was a crowd of
> something like 5,000 and more, have you any
> doubt that many of these people must have
> been unaware of your proclamation?
> A. It was being well issued and news spread very
> rapidly in places like that under prevailing
> conditions. At the same time there may have
> been a good many who had not heard the
> proclamation.
> Q. On the assumption that there was the risk of
> people being in the crowd who were not aware
> of the proclamation, did it not occur to you that
> it was a proper measure to ask the crowd to
> disperse before you took to actually firing upon
> them?
> A. No: at the time it did not occur to me. I
> merely felt that my orders had not been obeyed,

that martial law was flouted, and that it was my duty to immediately disperse it by rifle fire.

General Dyer also admits that it was quite possible that he could have dispersed them without firing.

Q. What reason had you to suppose that if you had ordered the assembly to leave the Bagh they would not have done so without the necessity of your firing, continued firing for a length of time?
A. Yes: I think it quite possible that I could have dispersed them perhaps even without firing.
Q. Why did you not adopt that course?
A. I could disperse them for some time, then they would all come back and laugh at me, and I considered I would be making myself a fool.

It is now admitted that among the 379 dead, now officially recognised, 87 were ascertained to be residents of outside villages. The proportion of the outside people in the meeting must have been appreciable as shown by the fact that it attracted the attention of General Dyer even within the extremely short time— 30 seconds—between his arrival and the opening of fire. He says in his report that the crowd appeared to be a mixed one, consisting of city people and outsiders.

It appears that the action of General Dyer was approved by General Beynon and also by Sir Michael O'Dwyer. General Beynon on the 14th April sent the following telegram:— "Your action correct. Lieutenant-Governor approves." Sir Michael O'Dwyer in his evidence before us, states that General

Beynon spoke to him over the telephone about the Jallianwala Bagh incident and said that he fully approved of it, and asked him (Sir Michael O'Dwyer) if he approved of it. Sir Michael O'Dwyer says that he at first said that it was not for him to criticise his (General Dyer's) action or to approve or disapprove of it. But General Beynon added that the situation in Amritsar had been completely restored. He (General Beynon) said that General Dyer would like to know that he (Sir Michael O'Dwyer) approved of his action. The entry in the War Diary of the 16th Division under date the 14th April is to the following effect:"At a conference at Government House, General Dyer's report on his action at Amritsar was considered and action taken was approved by the Lieutenant-Governor."

Sir Michael O'Dwyer told us that before General Beynon's telephonic message came on the 14th April, that morning he had got an account of the incident from the Deputy Commissioner which contained the information that General Dyer had fired without warning and had gone on firing for about 5 to 10 minutes and dispersed the crowd, inflicting 200 casualties, by which Sir Michael says he understood dead casualties. It was with this information before him that Sir Michael O'Dwyer expressed his approval of General Dyer's action later in the day.

We must say we are not surprised that Sir Michael O'Dwyer should have expressed such approval, for it appears from his evidence before us that he holds practically identical views with those of General Dyer in this matter. In his view, it did not matter if the people assembled at the Jallianwala Bagh that evening were different people from those who had committed murder and arson on the 10th, the very fact that they had assembled was enough to treat them as people who had committed murder and arson; and he also believes in the effect of General Dyer's action in crushing the alleged rebellion. In the written statement submitted to us he says: "The casualties were large and regrettable, but the loss of life was inevitable, when a truculent mob which had already committed murder and rebellion assembled to defy authority." The following extract from his *viva voce* examination is instructive:—

Q. I want to ask you a few questions about the Jallianwala Bagh incident. You say "the casualties were large and regrettable, but loss of life was inevitable when a truculent mob which had already committed murder and rebellion assembled to defy authority."

A. You have got my *addendum* to that statement.

Q. Yes, I will deal with that. The view there seems to be as if the crowd that had assembled there had committed murder and rebellion. Is there any evidence that that particular crowd had committed any murder or rebellion?

A. I do not suppose it could be said with reference to any particular crowd, but Amritsar city, as a whole, had committed murder and rebellion.

Q. You treated the whole city to be in rebellion, and therefore everybody in the city as taking part in that rebellion. That was your view.

A. The view I took there was that that meeting was held to show their hostility to Government and their sympathy with the people who had committed rebellion and murder.

Q. It may be that those who assembled there that evening may have been different people altogether from those who committed the actual murders and arson and other violent acts?

A. Yes, but they were there to show their sympathy with the people who committed murder and rebellion, and their hostility to the Government which was repressing it.

Q. There is no evidence to show that they assembled there for that?

A. I think it may be inferred from the fact that they had assembled there knowing what the conditions in Amritsar had been for the previous three days and knowing that any such meeting had been prohibited.

Q. I am coming to the prohibition. But there is no evidence to show that the assembly there expressed their sympathy with those who had committed murder and arson?

A. I think the fact that they had assembled there was enough; they would not have assembled there without good reason, at a critical time like that.

Q. The mere fact that they had assembled justified the conclusion that they had assembled there for the purpose of expressing sympathy?

A. I think after what had happened in Amritsar

for three days and taking that the prohibition issued that morning ...

Q. I am coming to the prohibition. You say they assembled to express sympathy. There is no evidence at all. You infer it?

A. Yes, I infer it.

At another place in his written statement, Sir Michael O'Dwyer says: —

"Speaking with perhaps more definite knowledge of the then situation than anyone else, I have no hesitation in saying that General Dyer's action was the conclusive factor in crushing the rebellion."

General Dyer wanted by his action at the Jallianwala Bagh to create a "wide impression" and "a great moral effect." We have no doubt that he did succeed in creating a very wide impression and a great moral effect, but of a character quite opposite to the one he intended. The story of this indiscriminate killing of innocent people not engaged in committing any acts of violence, but assembled in a meeting, has undoubtedly produced such a deep impression throughout the length and breadth of the country, so prejudicial to the British Government that it would take a good deal and a long time to rub it out. The action of General Dyer, as well as some acts of the martial law administration, to be referred to hereafter, have been compared to the acts of "frightfulness" committed by some of the German military commanders during the war in Belgium and France.

It is pleaded that General Dyer honestly believed that what he was doing was right. This cannot avail him, if he was clearly wrong in his notions of what was right and what was wrong; and the plea of military necessity is the plea that has always been advanced in justification of the Prussian atrocities. General Dyer thought that he had crushed the rebellion, and Sir Michael O'Dwyer was of the same view. There was no rebellion which required to be crushed. We feel that General Dyer, by adopting an inhuman and un-British method of dealing with subjects of His Majesty the King-Emperor, has done great disservice to the interest of British rule in India. This aspect it was not possible for the people of the mentality of General Dyer to realise. The following extract from his (General Dyer) evidence may be referred to in this connection: —

Q. Did it ever occur to you that by adopting this method of "frightfulness"—excuse the term—you were really doing a great disservice to the British Raj by driving discontent deep? A. No, it only struck me at the time it was my duty to do this and that it was a horrible duty. I did not like the idea of doing it, but I also realised that it was the only means of saving life and that any reasonable man with justice in his mind would realise that I had done the right thing; and it was a merciful act, though a horrible act, and they ought to be thankful to me for doing it.

Q. Did this aspect of the matter strike you that

by doing an act of that character you were doing a great disservice to the British Raj?
A. I thought it would be doing a jolly lot of good and they would realise that they were not to be wicked.

People like General Dyer have the fixed idea that the effective way of governing in India is force. It is the same idea that General Drake-Brockman of Delhi gave expression to in his written statement at Delhi: "Force is the only thing that an Asiatic has any respect for."

Treatment of the dead and wounded.

The conduct of General Dyer, after the firing was over, was in keeping with the attitude which dictated the firing. He immediately left the place with his troops and did not do anything to see that either the dead were attended to or the wounded received help. He did not consider it to be "his job". It is said that it would not have been quite safe for him to have stayed at the Bagh any longer, as there was the risk of the crowd that he had dispersed overpowering his force as his ammunition was finished. But for the purpose of arranging for the dead and the wounded, he need not have waited at the Bagh, but he could have given

the necessary directions for the purpose after reaching his headquarters at Ram Bagh. Either he was in
supreme command in supersession of the civil
authority or he was there in aid of the civil power. If
the former, we think he ought to have done
something about the matter. If the latter position was
the correct one, he should have informed the civil
authorities and they should have made the necessary
arrangements. But neither the civil nor the military
authorities seem to have done anything at all. The
following is General Dyer's evidence on the point: —

Q. After the firing had taken place did you take
any measure for the relief of the wounded?

A. No, certainly not. It was not my job. But the
hospitals were open and the medical officers were
there. The wounded only had to apply for help.
But they did not do this because they themselves
would be taken in custody for being in the
assembly. I was ready to help them if they applied.

Q. Were any measures taken immediately for
dealing with the dead?

A. They asked that they might bury their dead.

Q. That was much later?

A. My recollection is that when I got back they
came and asked me and I said certainly. It never
entered my head that the hospitals were not
sufficient for that number of wounded if they
had liked to come forward.

When General Dyer, in this part of his evidence,
said that when he got back, the people came and asked
that they might be allowed to bury the dead and he

gave the necessary permission, he was under a misapprehension. The asking and giving of such permission took place the next day, *viz.*, 14th April. In the report which General Dyer made of the operations from the 11th to 14th April to General Beynon, he, after narrating the Jallianwala Bagh incident, proceeds to say that he returned to the headquarters at 6 p.m. (13th) and at 10 p.m. he marched through the city to make sure that his orders as to the inhabitants not being out after 20 hours (13th) was obeyed; he found the city absolutely quiet and not a soul was to be seen. He then says, "the inhabitants have asked permission to bury the dead, and this I am allowing." This evidently refers to the 14th; the day on which he made the report. This is further borne out by the entry made by Captain Briggs in the War Diary about this permission. The order itself is dated the 14th April. When this was pointed out to General Dyer he admitted that the permission was given on the 14th of April.

As already stated above, Sir Michael O'Dwyer learnt on the 14th April from the Deputy Commissioner about the Jallianwala Bagh, that General Dyer had fired without warning and had gone on firing for about 10 minutes, and that there were 200 dead casualties. It does not appear that any steps were taken by the Punjab Government for a long time to ascertain the real facts about so serious an occurrence and to find out the correct number of casualties. Sir Michael O'Dwyer, when asked about it, says in his evidence that, on the 15th April he had an interview of about a quarter of an hour with General Dyer and that afterwards the Punjab Government were awaiting General Dyer's report. Sir Michael O'Dwyer said that in the latter part of April, General Dyer had been taking moveable columns to the various parts in the neighbourhood of Amritsar and that when he came back he was sent early in May to the Afghan War. General Dyer did not make his report till the end of August, 1919, and that was made in response to a communication from the Adjutant General dated the 19th July, 1919, evidently asking for a special report. The Punjab Government do not appear to have taken any steps till the end of June to ascertain the casualties. Mr. Thompson, the Chief Secretary, said: —

Q. Do you know what steps were taken to ascertain what the number of the causalities were?

A. There were no steps until about the end of July when we told the Deputy Commissioner to make inquiries.

It appears that notices were issued on the 8th of August, inviting people to give information regarding those who had met their death at the Jallianwala Bagh. During the discussion in the Imperial Legislative Council on the 19th September, 1919, in speaking about this matter the Government inquiries showed dead casualties to be 291, and that any information which puts the number beyond this should be received with the gravest caution.

In his evidence before us Mr. Thompson admitted that certainly 379 dead casualties had taken place, and that there was possibly still a small margin for more.

Administration of martial law: the "Crawling Order".

Among the orders passed by General Dyer at
Amritsar was an order that has been styled "Crawling
Order." This order was passed on the 19th April, eight
days after General Dyer arrived and four days after the
declaration of martial law. This order was passed with
reference to a street where Miss Sherwood had been
brutally attacked on the 10th April by the mob. The
street is narrow, but of considerable length, and has
abutting on it on both sides houses of different
dimensions. The order was to the effect that no

Indians should be allowed to pass through the street, but if they wanted to pass they must go on all fours, and pickets were placed at certain points in the street to enforce obedience to this order. The pickets had instructions to be there from 6 a.m. to 8 p.m. It is not suggested that the assailants of Miss Sherwood were the residents of the street. This order must have had the immediate result of seriously inconveniencing the residents of houses abutting on the street, and thereby punishing people who were *prima facie* innocent. General Dyer says he thought that all the houses had back entrances, but when one sees the street, as the Committee did, it is difficult to see how he carried that impression. Evidently it would not have affected his judgment or the order even if he had known that all the houses had no back entrances, for in his evidence before us, General Dyer seemed to think that it was really very slight inconvenience to the residents of the street. According to him they could go over the roofs of their houses. We are unable to understand how General Dyer expected the residents of these houses to go from the roof of one house to another, the houses being of different heights, and by that means reach the street.

Q. As I understand there are many houses with no back entrances at all?

A. I was not aware of that at the time.

Q. If it be the case that many of the houses have no back entrances what justification is there for pronouncing an order that necessitated the inhabitants lawfully residing in these houses to crawl on all-fours when they had to leave their homes?

A. They could leave at other times. My picket was only there from 6 a.m. to 8 p. m. I do not think it a very great inconvenience for them if they had to suffer a little for all that Amritsar had done. I thought it would be no harm under martial law. They could easily get the necessities of life by other means. It would not have taken much ingenuity to get necessary things. They might have suffered a little amount of inconvenience.

Q. How were they to get food, if most of the houses had no back entrances?

A. Those who had not back entrances, if they had to get the necessities of life, might have gone on the roof and improvised means. If not, they could wait until 8 o'clock in the night and then go out and get the things.

Q. All this thing might have a very different effect from the effect you wished. Instead of being a just punishment on those who were intended to be punished, it might cause a great deal of ill-feeling among those who resented treatment of this sort and who were not responsible for the acts that were done?

A. Amritsar had behaved very badly, and I think most of the inhabitants of Amritsar either gave assistance or were only waiting to see what was going to happen apparently. At any rate, they did not offer any help until after the firing, and if they suffered a little under martial law ...

Q. Do you admit that during a period of turmoil when the mob was having the upper hand, it is difficult for the peaceful citizen to give assistance in quelling the disturbances and it is just on that account that the extreme act of firing upon a mob is justified?

A. Yes, they were obstructing law-abiding citizens, I presume, but I think that on that occasion we only thought of punishing the wicked and men who had beaten Miss Sherwood who had to go through that street were punished. It was not my intention to punish anybody else.

General Dyer says that he did not expect that anybody would pass through the street and subject himself to this order of going on all fours. It was, however, a very curious coincidence that within a few minutes after he had passed the order and put the pickets, 12 persons had to be arrested for being insolent and he ordered them to be taken into custody, and the police took them through that street and the picket enforced the crawling order on them. General Dyer appears to have been pleased at this providential result. In his report he says: "I inspected the spot where Miss Sherwood ultimately fell, and I gave orders for a triangle to be erected there; I then posted two British pickets, one at each end of the street, with orders to allow no Indians to pass, that if they had to pass, they must go through on all fours. I never imagined that any sane man would voluntarily go through under those conditions, and I was still searching for some fitting punishment when Providence stepped in. After giving my orders I proceeded further through the city, and as I passed I gave orders for 11 insolent inhabitants to be handed over to the police, and brought to me at Ram Bagh at 9 a.m. next morning. I did not know that the police who accompanied my force had been left at the far end of the street in which the pickets were posted. Arriving at the near end of the street, the prisoners were confronted by the non-commissioned officer in command of the picket and made to crawl, between the two pickets, a distance of about 150 yards."

[The Sergeant in charge of the picket subsequently stated than one man "actually crawled through three times, and had to be stopped by the picket from giving further exhibitions."]

General Dyer further put up a triangle in this street for flogging people, and six persons who were under arrest in the fort for the assault on Miss Sherwood, on being found to have committed some breach of fort discipline, were brought and flogged there. These people were ultimately found guilty of the assault on Miss Sherwood, but at the time they were so flogged they were merely under-trial prisoners. There is no record forthcoming of the trial and punishments of the 11 persons above referred to, who were arrested for the breach of the salaaming order, or, of the other six persons who were flogged in the street.

Q. What certainty had you at the time you ordered them to be whipped at this spot that they would be found guilty of this offence against Miss Sherwood?

A. I did not know they would be found guilty, I lashed them.

Q. When they were lashed for a breach of Fort discipline they were not yet found guilty of the crime against Miss Sherwood—these particular men?

A. The chances were from what I heard and been told that these were the particular men. If they were not the particular men and another man was beaten, still it did not matter very much whether he was beaten there or somewhere else, if he was convicted. I did not wish to run the risk if he had committed the offence against Miss Sherwood, of his being beaten somewhere else; therefore, when I heard that these were the men, I had them beaten in the same street.

Q. Were you not rather doing that from the point of view of striking the popular imagination?

A. No, I had only that end in view that these men had in a dastardly manner beaten a woman and knocked her down six times in the street, and that nothing was too bad for them either from the point of view of a British man or a Hindu or a Sikh or any other man.

Sir Michael O'Dwyer strongly disapproved of this order and telephoned to General Beynon to have the order withdrawn as he considered it an improper order; and he informed the Viceroy as to what he had done in the matter.

Order requiring Indians to salaam European officers.

Among the martial law orders issued in the district, one attracts particular attention. That order which was issued on the 22nd April, required the inhabitants of the district whenever they met any gazetted European civil or military officer to show respect to them by alighting from any wheeled conveyance or animals that such inhabitants might be riding and close any open umbrellas that they might be carrying and to salute the said officers. This order was extended to the Lyallpur district on the 30th April and to the Gujrat district on the 2nd May. These orders were calculated to humiliate the whole Indian population of those districts and have naturally left much bitterness. In our view, the order, as it was issued and enforced, was wholly indefensible. Lieutenant-Colonel O'Brien says that he approved of the order: —

Q. Is it not enforcing humiliation on the Indian people, to make them alight from their carriages to salaam a European officer? Does it not savour of that?

A. You perhaps put the other way. It is rather this way. I go to the other extreme in insisting on the ordinary salutations being paid.

Q. It was necessary to go to the other extreme?

A. Perhaps so.

Q. For what purpose? What was the necessity for going to the other extreme and making this order?

A. The tendency of the present day is to abolish respectfulness. The Indian father will tell you that sons are not respectful even to their parents.

Q. The Indian young men are not following the ways of respectfulness and you therefore thought you would improve them by going to the other extreme and enforcing this order?

A. I say I did not pass this order. I generally agreed.

Q. That is the ground on which you defend it? I put it to you; if an order of this sort is in force would it not create considerable resentment and bitterness among the people, and would not they feel humiliated?

A. I do not know. The feeling of bitterness already existed.

Q. You thought there was bitterness sufficient and therefore any order of humiliation could not add to the bitterness?

A. I do not think its effect would be much.

PART TWO

∞◈◈∞

Disturbances in the Punjab.
Statement by Brig.-General R.E.H. Dyer, C.B.
Cmd. 771, 1920

From Brig.-General r.e.h. dyer, c.b.
To The Secretary,
War Office,
London, S.W.

33, Clarges Street, W.,
3rd July, 1920.

Sir,

In compliance with the permission given to me in War Office letter of 9th June, 1920, I have the honour to submit the statement which follows: —

1. Introduction and Statement of Issues

I necessarily assume that the action taken against me by the various authorities concerned is based on the report of and the proceedings before the Hunter Committee with regard to the events at Amritsar on or after the 11th April, 1919.

I assume this because I know of no other matters in respect of which any adverse comment has been made upon my conduct and because the Adjutant-General in India on 22nd March, 1920, when he personally informed me of the decision that I must resign my appointment, stated that the ground of the decision was that the Hunter Committee had reported adversely to me.

My present statement will therefore be confined in substance to defending myself against the adverse criticism of me contained in the report of the majority of the Hunter Committee, in the despatch of the Government of India, dated the 3rd May, 1920, forwarding the report to His Majesty's Government, and in the reply to that despatch by His Majesty's Government signed by the Secretary of State on the 26th May, 1920, both the latter being clearly founded upon material supplied by the Hunter Committee.

If I go occasionally outside these official criticisms it is only because I cannot wholly ignore some unofficial criticisms which have appeared in public, gravely detrimental to my reputation and which in justice to myself I must ask permission to deal with. I cannot, indeed, on the information before me ignore the possibility that such extraneous matters have influenced or may influence the action taken against me.

It is clear from the official documents above referred to that the main question I have to deal with is whether my action in dealing with the assembly in the Jallianwallah Bagh on the afternoon of the 13th April was too impetuous and too drastic.

Subsidiary questions are also raised (*a*) as to the omission to provide medical attendance for the wounded, and (*b*) as to the propriety of an order issued by me some days later regarding the use by natives of the street where Miss Sherwood was assaulted.

It is to the consideration of the judgments pronounced upon me regarding each of these matters that this statement is mainly devoted.

This is the first chance I have had of dealing with these criticisms, which I did not see till the recent publication of documents after my return home from India.

I wish to satisfy the Army Council that my action in these matters was justifiable, and that the criticisms are unfounded. I will do this as shortly as possible.

It will not, however, escape notice that in order to get exoneration from censure I am not called upon to go so far as to prove that at every stage I did right, nor is the Army Council called upon to take the burden upon itself of so deciding: all that is really necessary is for me to show that, situated as I was, I acted for the best and had reasonable ground for my action.

2. SUMMARY OF CHARGES IN REGARD TO FIRING IN JALLIANWALLAH BAGH

I will discuss the main question first.

The criticisms of my action in dealing with the crowd in the Jallianwallah Bagh may be shortly summarized as follows: —

(*a.*) Majority Report of the Hunter Committee.

The Committee blame me first for not giving a warning to the Assembly before I ordered fire to be opened so as to give people a chance to disperse. In continuing firing so long, the Committee hold that I committed a grave error, and that I had in view not merely the dispersal of the crowd that had assembled, but the desire to produce a moral effect in the Punjab, and that this was a mistaken conception of my duty, inasmuch as continued firing upon a crowd cannot be justified because of the effect such firing may have upon people in other places.

(*b.*) The despatch of the Government of India to the Secretary of State.

The Government of India declare that I could and should have given warning to the crowd before opening firing, that my action in continuing to fire after the crowd had begun to disperse was indefensible, and greatly exceeded the necessity of the occasion, and that I went beyond what any reasonable man could have thought to be necessary, and that I did not act with as much humanity as the case permitted.

(*c.*) The reply of the Secretary of State reiterates some of these criticisms and adds others.

It is there stated in particular that I acted in violation of the principle that the military when dealing with civil disturbances must use the minimum of force necessary, that the force I actually employed was greatly in excess of requirements, that my omission to give warning before fire was opened was inexcusable, that I had no right to punish an unarmed crowd which had not committed violence or tried to oppose me, and many members of which must have been ignorant of my orders, and that my conception of my duty was fundamentally at variance with that which the Government require from an officer.

3. Irregular and Prejudicial Method of Investigation

All these adverse criticisms are admittedly founded upon the report and proceedings of the Hunter Committee.

I must therefore, at the outset, point out to the Army Council that, however suitable those proceedings and report may have been as a guide to the formation of a general political opinion about the rebellion in India, and as an investigation of historical causes or of particular events, they were not such as to constitute in my case a judicial or regular enquiry into or trial of the conduct of an individual.

The wide terms of reference ("to investigate the recent disturbances in Bombay, Delhi and the Punjab, their causes and the measures taken to cope with them") hardly suggest that the trial of individuals was intended to be the function of the Committee.

In my case the procedure of a trial was not attempted. I received no notice of any charges against me. My official superiors had indeed up till then approved my conduct on the main question. I came and gave my evidence entirely unrepresented and undefended and in no sense expecting to find myself an accused person. I was present, except for a few hours on one casual occasion, during no part of the hearing of other witnesses, and apart from sometimes seeing newspaper summaries had no knowledge of what evidence they gave, or any opportunity to ask questions or elicit information, and no kind of address or argument was addressed to the Committee on my behalf. No member of the Committee constituted himself my advocate (it would clearly have been improper for any member to have done so), while several acted as my prosecutors, cross-examined me, and sought to establish a case against me, a course which their legal qualifications enabled them to pursue with special efficiency. I was furnished with no proof or transcript of my evidence, and had no opportunity to say anything by way of addition or qualification, or even to correct verbal inaccuracies. (Some of the phrases attributed to me I do not now recognise.) I never indeed saw my evidence or any of the criticisms of me until the recent publication of the Bluebook.

The anomalous result has been that I saw then for the first time and all at once charges, evidence and findings.

It is clear that this procedure was not in accordance with the course of justice normally observed at the hearing of complaints or charges against an individual.

It will be equally obvious to the Army Council that the procedure was wholly irregular according to military law and custom. A military court of enquiry, which is the normal method of investigating, if detailed investigation is needed, the conduct of an individual subject to military discipline requires his attendance throughout the proceedings, with the express object of assuring that he shall have full knowledge of any case which is being established against him, and an opportunity of dealing with charges suggested or evidence adduced adverse to him.

The case of a court-martial is still clearer, as then definite charges based on definite evidence have to be formulated in advance, and a proper opportunity has to be afforded for the preparation of the defence.

I do not wish to complain against the Committee for not adopting such a procedure. The scope and nature of its enquiry may not have permitted it. But in the absence of the normal requisites of a judicial investigation of the conduct of individuals, I ask that the Army Council will not regard the proceedings of the Committee as in any way conclusive, but will form its own judgment of my conduct as a soldier, giving due regard to the submissions which follow.

The Hunter Committee was, moreover, primarily and substantially a civil Committee. What is in question now is my conduct as an officer while administering martial law during a rebellion, and that should be judged by a military tribunal.

My treatment for nearly a year after the events at Amritsar further requires consideration. I had reported those events at once. Not only was I in no way criticised for my handling of the crisis, but I received immediate official approval. I was likewise in no way suspended from my duties, pending enquiry, the normal military course in the case of an officer whose conduct is to be the subject of censure or penalty. On the contrary I was promoted and also given a command on active service in the field.

I deal below more fully with the action of the military authorities in India at the time in approving my conduct or exonerating me from blame. I mention it here, because it demonstrates that I did not come before the Committee as an accused person, and had no occasion to provide myself with expert assistance in my absence.

The great delay before the enquiry started has likewise been a disadvantage to me, as officers and civilians who could have given important testimony had in the interval become unavailable. Criticisms publicly made by Sir Michael O'Dwyer of the complete suitability of the Committee to judge the Punjab Government should not be ignored in justice to myself as an agent of that Government.

4. THE PRINCIPLE OF "MINIMUM FORCE"
The principle is laid down by the Secretary of State

that an officer in suppressing civil disturbances must use the minimum amount of force necessary for the purpose. I am well acquainted with this principle, and have at all times fully accepted it. Quite apart from the ordinary experience of an officer of my seniority and length of service in the Indian Army, I had had special occasion and opportunity to study principles in this connection, as for five years I held the staff appointment of Deputy-Assistant Adjutant-General for instruction in military law, and the administration of martial law during civil disturbances was necessarily a subject of study by me in that capacity. I had this principle very clearly before me during the whole time I was in Amritsar, and I never at any time failed to act up to it to the best of my judgment and capacity. I say with all sincerity that I acted upon this principle when firing upon the assembly at Amritsar on the 13th April, and according to the best of my judgment (and no one was in a better position to judge than myself) I used no more force than was required by the occasion. This contention I hope to make good in what follows.

5. Statement of Situation and Narrative of Events

I now wish, as shortly as I can, to make clear the situation with which I was confronted in Amritsar, and the nature of the action which I took.

I will not again set out the history of the events which is told in the Hunter Report and recapitulated in the despatch of the Government of India and will only refer to the more important and significant features of the situation.

As military commander of the whole Jullundur district of which Amritsar is but one point, I was in touch with the general situation, and during the events which followed I was kept in touch also with the general situation in the Punjab. I had very recently toured through Delhi and other districts, and had been struck with the general unrest and the inflammable nature of many elements of the population. With the Sikh population of the countryside I was particularly well acquainted. The threatening nature of the Afghan situation was also present to me, also the weakness of the internal military situation and the threat to communications. To shorten this part of the narrative, I have summarized in a later paragraph the military considerations as they occurred to me.

On my arrival at Amritsar, on the evening of the 11th April, I was confronted with a crisis of the gravest kind. On the 10th the mob had risen, killed everyone of European nationality in the city upon whom it could lay hands, burned banks and Government buildings, and had been held off the European settlement outside the city only with the greatest difficulty. The situation had already been handed over to the local commander by the civil authorities as being a military one and beyond their control.

I found a clear conviction upon the part of the local officials and abundant signs that a determined

and organized movement was in progress to sub-
merge and destroy all the Europeans on the spot and
in the district and to carry the movement throughout
the Punjab, and that the mob in the city and the
excitable population of the villages were being organized for this purpose. In the end general looting and
mob violence against the whole law-abiding Indian
population as well as against the troops and authorities would have resulted.

For two days the city had been in the hands of the
mob, and no Government official or European could
enter it without an escort of troops. That in law and in
fact I was confronted not with a riot, but with open
rebellion, the Hunter Committee explicitly find.

The very restrained firing by troops and police
which had taken place on the 10th had produced no
effect at all, and the situation was more menacing
than ever.

There is much material in the official documents
to make clear the situation.

Admittedly Amritsar was the worst place concerned in the rebellion:

"The Amritsar incidents may be regarded as the
high water mark of the disorders" (Majority
Report).

The Secretary of State summarizes the situation
very clearly: —

"In Amritsar itself violence, murder and arson of
the most savage description had occurred three
days previously, and the city was still practically

in the possession of the mob. From the surrounding countryside reports were hourly being received of violent similar outbreaks and attacks upon communications, and the deficiencies in these reports (due to the success of attacks upon communications) were supplemented by rumours which there was very little means of verifying and as little ground for disbelieving." (*Despatch*, page 24.)

I had only a small force of troops at my disposal consisting of at the outset 475 British and 710 Indian, many of them only partially trained. Amritsar is a city of 150,000 people, and the countryside is densely populated with a people of an inflammable character. The arrangement of the city and the civil lines did little to facilitate the problems of control and defence.

The signs which met me and the reports which I received left no doubt as to the existence of an organized mob with leaders, and a definite purpose of outrage and destruction.

The organization of mobs in Amritsar had been noticeable at a much earlier stage when violence was not expected.

Speaking of the organization of the initial agitation about the 6th April, Mr. Miles Irving, the Deputy-Commissioner, Amritsar, gave evidence as follows: —

Q. After the 6th, how did the situation strike you?

A. They were working up for some kind of mischief which I could not foresee. It struck me that the leaders of the movement were disciplining the mob with a view to some concerted form of passive disobedience to authority which would paralyse Government.

Q. But so far as any immediate act of violence is concerned did you see anything that was being encouraged?

A. My idea was that they intended to avoid any collision with authority that would justify Armed intervention and to train the mob to do what they were told. (Evidence Vol. III, page 3)

When, contrary to previous expectation, violence broke out, such organization quickly showed itself, and as Mr. Irving said later (page 11, Vol. III, Evidence) we found by experience there was sufficient organization down in the lowest stratum to go and spread with wonderful rapidity to do acts of violence. The formation of "Bludgeon Armies" (Danda Fauj) was a common matter of rebel propaganda, and the vast supplies of bludgeons which we intercepted on the railway a few days later were indications of the designs of the revolutionaries.

The events of the 12th and early part of the 13th April may be stated here in the summary afterwards given to the legislative Council by the Adjutant-General in his speech of the 19th September, 1919:—

"On the 11th and 12th he (Brigadier-General Dyer) reorganized his troops and on the 12th he marched a column round and through the city in order that a display of force might have its effect on the minds of the populace. We have it on record that the bearing of the inhabitants was most insolent, and that many spat on the ground as the troops passed. From the shouts of the mob it was clear that they were in an entirely unrepentant spirit. No military force was used on this occasion as the officer in command decided to issue proclamations as to his future intentions before employing such force. From a military point of view he would have been quite justified, I hold, in using force on that day, but the General Officer Commanding decided to pursue his policy of patience and conciliation. A proclamation was issued on the evening of the 12th, and on the morning of the 13th April the Officer Commanding marched with a body of troops through all the main streets of the city and announced by beat of drum his intentions of using force should occasion arise. The people were permitted to collect in order to hear the proclamations." (*Official Report*, 19th September, 1919, page 376)

Reference should also be made to the report of my Brigade-Major, Captain F. C. C. Briggs, D.S.O., which gives a succinct account of events at this stage.

The prohibition of assemblies in time of riot and disturbance is an elementary and well understood expedient in India, and no question is raised as to the justification for my proclamation or the announcement that any assembly gathering in defiance of it would be dispersed by force of arms. (The Hunter Committee say of a similar order issued at Ahmedabad that "the belief that all groups of more than 10 men would be fired on without warning did much to restore order.")

The method of issuing it, namely, the progress for $4\frac{1}{2}$ hours of a body of troops about the city accompanied by the General himself and the Deputy-Commissioner, the summoning of the population by beat of drum, and the reading of it in two languages as they assembled, was itself an unusual and significant demonstration.

I hoped it would be sufficient to do something to quiet the situation.

But it was answered by an immediate challenge. I gradually learnt on my return to the civil lines that a counter-proclamation had been issued behind me, that the rumour had been set going that my action was mere pretence, and that I dared not fire, and that a meeting would be held in the Jallianwallah Bagh in the afternoon. Later the news came that the meeting was actually assembling.

I explain my motives and beliefs during the action which followed more fully below. Here it is sufficient to say that I know that the final crisis had come, and that the assembly was primarily of the same mobs which had murdered and looted and burnt three days previously, and showed their truculence and contempt of the troops during the intervening days, that it was a deliberate challenge to the Government forces, and that if it were not dispersed, and dispersed effectively, with sufficient impression upon the designs and arrogance of the rebels and their followers we should be overwhelmed during the night or the next day by a combination of the city gangs and of the still more formidable multitude from the villages. A crowd from the city of 30,000 had menaced the civil settlement on the 10th. Its audacity in the meantime had grown with its crimes and their immunity. The villages had been brought in, and I had to reckon upon the possibility of the irruption that night of some 30,000 Majha Sikh looters, if the whole movement were not decisively checked. As an illustration of the facts before me the following passage from Mr. Irving's evidence will be sufficient here: —

Q. Did you form any opinion as to what the intention of the mob was with reference to Government?

A. The mob in the Jallianwala?

Q. Generally speaking the mob in Amritsar, from the 10th to the 13th April?

A. I believe it seriously thought it had a chance of beating the Government. One of the ringleaders, when he was talked to, said, "well, let us have the fight out". That was somewhere between the 10th and 18th, when he was being talked to by a friendly Indian gentleman; that is what he said, I believe.

Q. Do you understand that to mean a fight out

between the populace on the one hand and organized authority on the other?

A. Yes. (Evidence, Vol. III, page 7.)

I took the small force at my disposal, consisting of the picquetting parties and a special party consisting of 25 rifles 1/9th Gurkhas, 25 rifles 54th Sikhs, and 59th Sikhs and 40 Gurkhas armed only with kukries, and two armoured cars, and after dropping some necessary pickets arrived about 5 p. m. in the Jallianwallah Bagh with the special party, none of them at all highly trained men. I entered it at one end by a narrow passage, through which my armoured cars could not pass.

I found a large meeting, afterwards ascertained to be from 15,000 to 20,000 in number, being addressed by a speaker engaged in violent exhortation. The speakers at this meeting were in fact most, if not all, of them later convicted of sedition in connection with the disturbances. There were no women and children in the meeting, and its appearance confirmed the reports I had received as to its character.

The position was itself an anxious one from a purely military point of view—of the other aspects I speak below—as I was liable to be assailed from behind, and the extrication of my small force from the city would have been practically impossible if after the firing the rebels had maintained an aggressive spirit.

Hesitation I felt would be dangerous and futile, and as soon as my fifty riflemen had deployed I ordered fire to be opened. The crowd began to scatter to the various exits. After some firing two groups appeared to be collecting as though to rush us, and on my Brigade-Major calling my attention to this I directed fire specially to the two points in question, and dispersed the groups. When 1,650 rounds or thereabouts had been fired, and roughly ten minutes from the time of opening fire, the whole crowd had dispersed, and I was able to lead the body of troops back in security, having, as it turned out, established general security in Amritsar and the neighbourhood for everyone. The spirit of the organized mobs was effectively broken, and the unrest in the countryside stopped.

I reported my action to Divisional Headquarters next day, describing briefly the events above set out, and stated that I estimated the dead casualties at between 200 and 300. I received from the Divisional Commander by aeroplane the message, "Your action correct, and Lieutenant-Governor approves."

Subsequent enquiries, according to the Hunter Committee, put the number of dead at 379, but of such enquiries I have no information.

6. CONNECTION BETWEEN ARMITSAR AND REST OF PUNJAB AND RESULTS OF FIRING

Before discussing the above proceedings in relation to the adverse criticisms upon them, I would say a word as to the connection between the events in Amritsar and the rest of the Punjab.

It was, as will be seen, very close. First, as to the

rebellious movement itself. Before I left Jullundur I was well aware of the effect of the outrages of the 10th April in Amritsar upon the districts outside.

The Hunter Committee leaves no doubt as to the fatal progress of events. Of the situation at Lahore, which clearly became nearly as threatening as that at Amritsar, the Committee says "that on the 10th the political atmosphere, already highly charged, was made acutely worse by the arrival of two pieces of news, one the arrest of Mr. Gandhi, and the other the news of the horrible outbreak at Amritsar."

A poster in the vernacular issued in Lahore exhorted imitation of Amritsar as follows.

"When the news (*i.e.*, of Mr. Gandhi's arrest) reached Amritsar, the Danda Fauj (Bludgeon Army) of the brave Sikhs set fire to the Bank, the Railway Station and Electric Power House. They cut the telegraph wires and removed the railway line. The Danda Fauj of Amritsar bravely killed a number of European monkeys and their Sikh regiments have revolted and deserted. O Hindu, Muhammedan and Sikh brethren enlist at once in the Danda Army and fight with bravery against the English monkeys. God will grant you victory . . ."

Of Patti, a town in the Lahore district, and about 28 miles from Amritsar, the Committee find that:—

"The news of the Amritsar disorders on the 10th disposed the Patti mob towards loot."

The outbreak at Gujrianwala was clearly serious. Describing its progress, the Committee say: —

"Until the news of the happenings of the 10th at Amritsar and Lahore had time to affect the people of Gujrianwala there seems to have been no intention to hold a second hartal. After that news Europeans and authorities were alike naturally apprehensive."

and again:—

"The main object of the mob was certainly to destroy all Government buildings and there is little room for doubt that they were imitating or repeating what they heard of Amritsar on the 10th."

and again:—

"At Sheikhupura on the 12th there were processions and excited speeches containing descriptions of the events at Lahore and Amritsar."

Next, as to the effect of my action in the Jallianwallah Bagh on the afternoon of the 13th. The evidence as to this is copious and conclusive. Of the effect in Amritsar itself, the evidence of Mr. Miles Irving leaves no room for doubt:—

Q. What was the result of this firing on that mob?
A. The whole rebellion collapsed. Not only the mob that was fired upon naturally dispersed and all trouble ceased in the city of Amritsar, but it

was felt throughout the district. One of the reasons why there had been a danger was that the people not in the district thought for some reason or other that the Arm of Government was paralysed. The inaction of the police when the National Bank was burned lent some colour to that belief and there was an idea that the Government could do nothing, and this came as a disillusionment.

And Major-General Benyon in his report says:—

"(iv.) The wisdom of General Dyer's action has been fully proved by the fact that there has been no further trouble of any sort in Amritsar. The news had a decidedly sobering effect on the surrounding villages when it spread to them."

With regard to the effect generally, Sir Michael O'Dwyer, the Lieutenant-Governor, whose judgment on such a matter was necessarily the best, stated: —

"I have no hesitation in saying that General Dyer's action that day was the decisive factor in crushing the rebellion, the seriousness of which is only now being realised."

The evidence of Lieutenant-Colonel Johnson, commanding the troops at Lahore who plainly had to face there a situation of the utmost gravity is exceptionally significant. He told the Committee (at page 26 of Vol. IV of the Evidence (Lahore and Kasur)):—

Q. Therefore I think your opinion is that these were the very things which practically maintained peace and order—these Martial Law orders?

A. I put four things forward why peace was maintained and bloodshed avoided. First of all about 60 per cent I put to General Dyer's action at Amritsar; the next thing I put to the institution of Martial Law; the third thing, I had a sufficient number of troops placed at my disposal here; and the fourth—and a very minor consideration—was the use that one made of that power and those troops—

15 per cent for the number of troops.
20 per cent for Martial Law.
60 per cent for General Dyer.
5 per cent for the use made of powers and men.

Now General Dyer had proclaimed his own Martial Law which he was prepared to do. Whether Martial Law was proclaimed or not is a common factor.

Q. You mean then that when the news of what had happened on the 13th at Amritsar arrived at Lahore the situation was eased and things were looking better?

A. Yes, there was a change in the atmosphere.

Q. Therefore, that was due to the action of General Dyer? May I know whether there was any opportunity for such communication between Amritsar and Lahore?

A. I should think every means of communication barring the telegraph, motor bicycles, &c., I cannot imagine there would have been difficulty in the way of communication.

Q. If you accept this proposition that what happened on the 13th would not reach Lahore—under the circumstances that were prevailing on the 14th—will you be prepared to modify your statement?

A. It did reach Lahore on the 13th. It was common property late that night.

And General Beynon says: —

"The strong measures taken by General Dyer at Amritsar had a far-reaching effect and prevented any further trouble in the Lahore Divisional area."

On page 9 of their despatch the Government of India say: —

"It is more than probable that General Dyer's action so intimidated the lawless elements in the population of Amritsar and neighbouring districts of the central Punjab as to prevent further manifestations of disorder"

and

"we think that in the result his (General Dyer's) action at the time checked the spread of the disturbances to an extent which it is difficult now to estimate. This was the opinion of many intelligent observers in the Punjab."

I will only remark here that I cannot understand how it can be suggested that the objects of crushing the rebellion in Amritsar or elsewhere, of diminishing the dangers in Lahore by 60 per cent, of intimidating the lawless elements in the population of Amritsar and neighbouring districts, and preventing further manifestations of disorder, and of checking the spread of disturbances were not proper objects upon which to employ a military force during a rebellion.

If they were proper objects, the Hunter Committee supply no evidence or arguments to show that I employed any more force than was necessary to secure them.

The whole gravamen of the Committee's case against me is indeed not that I used excessive force to secure these objects, but that they were not proper objects for me to endeavour to secure.

The Committee could hardly have ruled that the casualties were out of proportion to the general situation to be faced or to the actual results achieved, if once they were willing to assume that I was entitled to face the situation and to seek to achieve the results, when their own appreciation of that situation is considered: —

> "In the situation as it presented itself day by day to the Punjab Government there were grounds for the gravest anxiety. Within recent years there had been two revolutionary movements, i.e., the Ghadr movement and the Silk Letter Conspiracy of 1916. It was difficult, probably

unsafe for the authorities not to assume that the outbreak was the result of a definite organization. Apart from the existence of any deeply laid scheme to overthrow the British, a movement which had started in rioting and become a rebellion might have rapidly developed into a revolution."

"As a description of the occurrences to which we have called attention in our narrative of events, 'open rebellion' is, we think, apt and accurate; as a question of inference it appears to us to be the natural and the only inference. The element of rebellion as distinct from mere riot on the one hand and from political opposition to Government on the other can be traced throughout; in what sense it may be considered to lack openness we have failed to discover ...

... On 10th April at Amritsar the mobs had burned Government buildings because they were Government buildings. After the first few minutes they had murdered all Europeans on whom they could lay their hands, except Miss Sherwood, whom they left for dead upon the street. They had hunted for Mrs. Easdon and the officers of the Chartered Bank; the other bank managers were sought out in their offices and killed with every circumstances of brutal rage. They were not even Government officials. But the Raj is a British Raj; they were in some sense its representative or symbols, and for this they were murdered. The railway and the telegraphs were attacked partly as Government institutions and partly to paralyse Government by preventing news, by derailing troops, and otherwise immobilizing the forces.

The Amritsar incidents may be regarded as the high water mark of the disorders though the outbreak at Kasur on the 12th is hardly distinguishable."

We know that the Secretary of State considers that the Committee's appreciation of the danger is, if anything, below the mark. Can it be suggested that the casualties caused by my action on the 13th April were out of proportion to the result—the suppression of such a rebellion?

7. REPLY TO THE CHARGE OF EXCESSIVE FORCE AND EXPLANATION OF MOTIVES

I will now proceed to deal briefly and directly with the Committee's criticisms and to explain, as clearly as I can, the precise motives of my action.

I say frankly at the outset that if the above described objects were not proper objects for me to seek in my action against the crowd in the Jallianwallah Bagh, then, on the major point, I may be open to criticism, and can only plead that I acted according to my best judgment under a mistaken sense of duty.

If these were right objects to pursue, I submit that, on the major point there is no case against me.

I put [*one after the other*] an extract from my own report and the vital comment of the Committee.

Extract from my own Report

"I fired and continued to fire until the crowd dispersed, and I consider this is the least amount of firing which would produce the necessary moral and widespread effect it was my duty to produce if I was to justify my action. If more troops had been at hand, the casualties would have been greater in proportion. It was no longer a question of merely dispersing the crowd, but one of producing a sufficient moral effect from a military point of view not only on those who were present, but more especially throughout the Punjab. There could be no question of undue severity."

Comment of the Committee

"In our view, this was unfortunately a mistaken conception of his duty. If necessary, a crowd that has assembled contrary to a proclamation issued to prevent or terminate disorder may have to be fired upon; but continued firing upon that crowd cannot be justified because of the effect such firing may have upon people in other places. The employment of excessive measures is as likely as not to produce the opposite result to that desired."

With the last sentence of the Committee's opinion no one will quarrel. The essential point, however, is that contained in the words, "continued firing upon that crowd cannot be justified because of the effect such firing may have upon people in other places." I believe the Army Council will repudiate with emphasis the principle involved in these words as being an abstract principle which cannot possibly govern the particular crisis with which I was confronted or any similar crisis.

The principle in the only sense in which it is relevant to or supports the criticism of my action comes to this—that my sole right was to secure the purely mechanical effect of causing the crowd to move off from the place where it was and go resolved into its individual elements to some other place or places. What it might do wherever it or its elements went was no concern of mine. The fact that it might go off full of derision and contempt of my force to burn and loot elsewhere, or to surround and overwhelm my troops as they moved out of the city, was not to influence my action at all. In fact, none of the possible consequences of leniency were to be considered at all.

I invite repudiation of this principle on three grounds (among others): first, that the Hunter Committee do not themselves adopt any such principle in dealing with other cases in their report; secondly, that the principle is repudiated by the Secretary of State for India, in his despatch; and thirdly, that the principle is wrong.

(*a*.) The recognition by the Committee itself in other cases that an officer when firing on a crowd may look beyond the needs of the movement is clear.

On page 1 of the report in regard to Delhi: —
> "firing continued no longer than was necessary
> to achieve the legitimate object of restoring
> order and preventing a disastrous outbreak of
> violence."

On page 16 of the same report the Committee
say (with reference to Niagram in the Ahmedabad
district): —
> "the force used against the rioters ... was cer-
> tainly not excessive. If greater force could have
> been applied at an early stage, the commission of
> an atrocious murder and much destruction of
> property might have been prevented."

and on page 38 (with reference to the disorders at
Lahore): —
> "we think that it was essential on this day to
> disperse this crowd, and that it would have been
> the end of all chance to restore order in Lahore
> if the police and troops had left without
> dispersing it."

As regards Gujrianwala, the Committee clearly
consider that the accident of the recent departure of
the Deputy Commissioner (Colonel O'Brien)
resulted in the situation being too weakly handled; on
page 45 they say: —
> "in failing to order the police to fire upon and so
> disperse these mobs around the burning post
> office the acting Deputy Commissioner (at
> Gujrianwala) appears to us to have committed an

error. If effective measures had then been taken
to disperse the mob and restore order, the later
incidents of the day might have been avoided."

It is, I think, a legitimate comment that officers
who deal with disturbances in future are placed in a
great difficulty by these different rulings. If they consider only the immediate needs of the moment, they
are liable to be condemned for not looking further
ahead and for ill consequences which occur elsewhere and later. If they do as I did and consider the
situation as a whole and act with a view to restore
order and to prevent further outbreaks, they are liable
to be told that they must not look beyond the dispersal of the crowd at the moment.

(*b*.) The despatch of the Secretary of State gives
no countenance to the view that I was required to
look at events in isolation and disregard consequences
in the action which I took.

"They (His Majesty's Government) think it is
possible that the danger to the lives of
Europeans and to the safety of British and
Indian troops was greater than appears from the
Committee's report ... [Then follows the
passage about the conditions in Amritsar and the
neighbourhood, and continues]: In discharging
this responsibility with the small force at his
disposal, Brigadier-General Dyer naturally could
not dismiss from his mind conditions in the
Punjab generally, and he was entitled to lay his
plans with reference to those conditions."

(*c*.) Thirdly, I say that the basis of criticism adopted by the Committee is on the face of it wrong and contrary to common sense. An officer dealing with riots is bound to consider consequences, and if faced with a rebellious gathering to consider what may happen both then and thereafter, both in that place and any other places affected or likely to be affected by the same movement, according as he lets the gathering alone or disperses it, or according as he disperses it effectively or ineffectively, *e.g.*, leaving it with its defiance and designs unaffected, and its power for mischief unreduced. The measures he takes must depend on circumstances. Extreme dangers justify strong measures. He must in any case be largely judged by results.

As to people in other places, I did not wish to influence people or places that were not affected or in danger of being affected by the rebellion, but only the people who were involved or were becoming involved in the same movement in the neighbourhood of Amritsar and in other places in the Punjab.

It is, of course, impossible for me to separate the effect of these various considerations, and say what I should have done if one or other had not been present, whether, *e.g.*, if Amritsar had been merely an isolated incident and not the storm centre of the Punjab, or if the danger from the countryside, our constant pre-occupation, could have been ignored, I should have acted precisely as I did. I looked at the realities of the case as a whole, as a soldier was bound to do.

But if any one dominant motive can be extracted it was the determination to avert from the European women and children and those of the law-abiding Indian community the fate which I was convinced would be theirs, if I did not meet the challenge and produce the required effect to restore order and security. I am conscious that it was this motive which gave me the strength of will to carry out my duty. Of its force in the mind of an Indian Army officer of thirty-four years' residence in India I am sure the Army Council will have no doubt. The terms of the thanks which I afterwards received from so many Indians showed what a cloud of apprehension rested upon the minds not only of Europeans but of the law–abiding Indian population as a whole regarding the fate of their children and women-folk during those fateful days.

Upon the above considerations, I submit that if my object be admitted to be a proper object, namely, the restoration of order and security, and if I was not confined to the bare mechanical operation of getting the crowd "to move on," then no evidence or ground is anywhere suggested to show that the force I used was in the least degree excessive. The Committee do not indeed anywhere attempt to show this, but base their disapproval substantially on the ground that I had no right to seek the general object of the restoration of order, but should have confined myself to the bare mechanical operation above mentioned.

Upon the assumption that I was justified in seeking the wider object, and in the absence of any ground shown for regarding my action as excessive upon that assumption, I will only allude to the adverse comments made in other parts of the Committee's report upon officers who took insufficient action to secure the wider object of the restoration of order, and to the complete ineffectiveness of the measures taken in Amritsar on the 10th.

As regards the latter point the Adjutant-General speaking before the Legislative Council five months later, was quite clear: —

> "Now he (Brig.-General Dyer) was well aware of the events of 10th April when the murders of Europeans and the attacks on property had been made, and when the firing which had been employed to suppress these disorders had been totally inadequate."

I am not here reflecting upon the authorities in charge of Amritsar before my arrival on the evening of the 11th April. At the time of the firing in question, the nature and extent of the outrages were not known to them. But the results which appeared afterwards and were presented to me on my arrival showed how ineffective the action taken had in fact been.

In the same connection I may quote the Committee's own comment on the firing by the small picket near the Hall Bridge on the 10th April:—

> "It angered some, and as an incitement it might well be effective with others."

In point of fact, after this first firing, the crowd merely withdrew from the point assailed, and proceeded to attack and smash up the telegraph office, and attempt the murder of the telegraph master, who was rescued only at the last moment by the station picket.

8. POINTS AS TO PUBLICITY OF PROCLAMATION AND LACK OF WARNING TO CROWD

It will be convenient that I should deal separately with two subsidiary points which arise in connection with my action in dispersing the mob on the 13th and have been made the subject of criticism: —

(*a*.) That I did not cause my proclamation in the early part of the day to be sufficiently published;

(*b*.) That I failed to give a further warning to the crowd before I actually caused fire to be opened upon it.

I think that I am justified in saying that neither the Hunter Committee nor the Government of India regard either of these points as involving questions of much practical moment, and I believe their importance will be found to lie in the inference which the Secretary of State has allowed himself to draw from them, inferences which I respectfully submit will be found on further consideration to involve a substantial misunderstanding of the facts.

(*a*.) As regards the publication of the proclamation, the Committee do not allege that the proclamation was not advertised as widely as was reasonably possible, and consider that most of those who were present at the meeting were aware of it. They say:

> "the majority of the people who assembled had done so in direct defiance of a proclamation issued in the interests of peace and order, many thinking that the reference to firing was mere bluff."

The Government of India say:

> "it cannot therefore be doubted that most of the residents of Amritsar present at the meeting were aware of the orders and collected in defiance of them."

The Secretary of State also does not appear, in the first instance, to attach much importance to this point taken by itself as he says:

> "It would be unfair, considering the state of the city, the heat of the weather and the strain to which the troops ... have been subjected ... to lay too great stress upon this point" (namely, that the proclamation was published in a portion of the city only).

I trust that the account I have already given and the comments I have already made on the situation will make it clear that I, at the moment of action, entertained the belief and had proper ground for believing that substantially everyone in the crowd knew that he had assembled in defiance of orders issued, and was there with a defiant and revolutionary intent. At the risk of some repetition I will emphasize a few grounds for this belief.

The general understanding in India that in times of riot crowds are not allowed to assemble must itself not be left out of account.

Next, quite apart from my own proclamation, the orders of the authorities had been clearly indicated throughout the two preceding days when crowds had been repeatedly ordered to disperse. This happened several times during the 12th, when, as the Adjutant-General afterwards said, I should have been justified in firing, but I refrained from doing so.

Moreover my proclamation of the 13th was not the only one. A previous proclamation prohibiting assemblies and declaring that all gatherings would be fired on had been drawn up by the Deputy Commissioner and issued on the 11th April by being given to a number of citizens to be published as best they could, and on the 12th I caused another to be issued by the police.

With regard to the actual issue of my own proclamation on the 13th, the evidence of the Deputy Commissioner, Mr. Miles Irving shows what happened. From 9 a.m. to about 1.30 p.m. I led a column through the streets of the city, accompanied by him. The column was halted at about 18 distinct places where drums were beat in order to collect the people and where the proclamation was read after people had collected. The proclamation was read out in the official Urdu language and also explained in Punjabee language to the common people. That it was heard by and known to the riotous element in the city was shown by their immediate issue of a counter procla-

mation, the effect of which was to publish my proclamation still further. The Deputy Superintendent of
Police, Mr. Plomer, says that, after I had made my
proclamation, three persons went round beating an
empty Kerosene tin announcing that the meeting
would be held in the Jallianwallah Bagh, in deliberate
defiance of my order.

I need scarcely say that the mere procession of a
body of troops round the city accompanied by the
General himself and the Deputy Commissioner
would be a demonstration of unusual significance and
attracting general attention.

Lastly, while I throughout this difficult business
have done my best to keep my own responsibility to
the fore, I had to follow, as regards the places where
the proclamation should be published, the guidance
of the local official who knew the city of Amritsar,
with which I personally was little acquainted.

News travels with the utmost quickness in a place
like Amritsar and the surrounding neighbourhood,
and speaking from my 34 years of experience, I have
no hesitation in saying that the order against crowds
and the threat to fire was as well known as anything
could have made them by the afternoon.

(*b.*) With regard to the criticism that I failed to
warn the crowd before firing, it is to be noticed
that the Hunter Committee concede that a particular military situation (*e.g.*, the risk of a small force
of soldiers being overwhelmed by a threatening
mob) may justify firing without the formality of

giving a notice to disperse being observed, and that the only person who can judge whether or not such an emergency has arisen is the officer in command of the troops. As I said in my report to my divisional commander, I realized that my force was small and untrained, and that to hesitate might induce attack, and if I had reasonable grounds for my view I am brought within the reservation made by the Committee. But, apart from the imminent danger it was, in my view, futile and unnecessary to address the crowd because I was satisfied that it was a rebellious gathering, and knew of the proclamations that had been issued and had assembled in defiance of them, and that no warning would induce them to disperse. The actual approach of the troops, a comparatively slow process, must obviously have been heralded to the crowd by runners, and thereby itself operated as a warning. The Committee take the view that

> "It is distinctly improbable ... that the crowd ...
> would have dispersed upon notice being made
> that they should do so, and much more likely
> that recourse to firing would have been necessary
> to secure obedience to the proclamation."

And the Government, India say that—
> " ... in view of this circumstance (the smallness
> of my force) and the previous successes of the
> forces of disorder, it is most improbable that an
> excited and defiant mob would have dispersed
> on a mere warning."

The facts already stated with regard to the publication of the proclamation and the other warnings issued against meetings, and what I myself saw of the character of the crowd with no women or children in it, were sufficient to convince me of the utter futility of any further proclamation. That it was guided and addressed by criminal revolutionaries I felt sure, and events have proved that I was right. Quite apart from the military danger to which I have alluded, the spectacle of this dense crowd under such circumstances and listening to such speakers was enough to convince anyone on the spot that further warning was not a practical requirement of the situation.

I can see now that, if I had been thinking of protecting myself from subsequent attacks, I might have given more attention to the matter, but the needs of the immediate situation and not protecting myself from subsequent criticisms were my guide.

9. CROWD NOT INNOCENT AS SUGGESTED BY SECRETARY OF STATE

I think that the real importance to my case of the two foregoing matters lies in the indirect influence they have had upon the Secretary of State.

After referring at a later stage of his Despatch to my omission to give warning before actually ordering fire to be opened as being inexcusable, he concludes his comment: —

"But he was not entitled to select for condign punishment an unarmed crowd, which, when he inflicted that punishment, had committed no act of violence, had made no attempt to oppose him by force, and many members of which must have been unaware that they were disobeying his commands."

The ground of criticism here is changed. The principle of the Hunter Committee that I was not entitled to look beyond the needs of the moment and the mere removal of the crowd from the Bagh has (as already explained) been discarded. With the different principle embodied on the above comment I respectfully concur. To produce the impression upon a rebellious population required to restore order by deliberately firing upon an innocent gathering would have been indefensible.

Such an idea never entered into my head. What I have already said will, I trust, make clear that I was faced with no such gathering, but with a defiant, organized, and rebellious mob, with a record of at least two days of outrage and treason behind it and the above vital comment of the Secretary of State is based upon imperfect information as to the facts. The Government of India certainly do not take his view of the facts, as they speak in the extract above recited of "an excited and defiant mob."

The expert prosecution of me, facilitated by the absence of any expert defence, I have already mentioned. The skilful extraction of passages from my evidence to be used against me, the reference to "people of the mentality of General Dyer" and the conclusion directed both against Sir Michael O'Dwyer as well as myself that "there was no rebellion which required to be crushed" show the nature of the hostility with which, for the first time after months of official approval or exoneration, I found myself faced.

I should make this statement too long if I were to go through the report and deal with its various charges, and I have not attempted to do so. But I am compelled to mention it here, as it is possible that it is to some extent reflected in the present criticism with which I am dealing. I notice in particular the phrase "indiscriminate killing of innocent people not engaged in committing any acts of violence". One of the Minority Committee, in a question to a witness, even described the meeting as a "lecture".

I have said, I trust, enough to show the absurdity of the view that I was faced with an ordinary political assembly composed of non-criminal elements. But, in view of the apparent adoption by the Secretary of State of this "innocent" theory, I may be allowed to deal with two further points in connection with it.

The presence in the crowd of villagers from outside the city appears to be thought important, as showing that people to whom the proclamation had not been read were involved.

So far as the question of knowledge is concerned, I submit on the facts previously stated, that there would be a general knowledge throughout Amritsar and all natives visiting it that meetings were prohibited.

So far as the question of motive is concerned, the presence of the villagers only made the matter more sinister. I was aware that the day was one of a fair and a festival. I was aware, too, of the continued efforts of the agitators beneath the surface to bring the villages into the rebellion. It was here that the worst danger really lay. Even if they came into the city with innocent motives, they would find it seething with the murderous triumphs and treasonable defiance of the two previous days. But there was only too much reason to fear that they would come with no innocent motive and Sikh looters from without would have been infinitely more dangerous than the city mob. The Deputy-Commissioner (Mr. Irving) gave significant evidence on this side of the matter:—

Q. Then on the 13th, the situation continued critical?

A. It continued very critical. We were able to hold the outskirts of the city. We made no impression in the city. The city was still impenitently hostile and that was not the worst, because the great danger was from the outside. If the villagers of the Manjha had turned loose, we should have had a situation not paralleled since the Mutiny. We know them to be hot-headed men, who, if they thought that the Government was failing, would step in for anything they could get.

Q. Can you say yourself whether any rumours were afloat as regards general looting?
A. I was informed that the rumour in the villages was that there was any amount of loot in Amritsar. Government was failing in the control of the situation and the sooner people came in to get their share, the better. It was brought out in evidence that in certain villages people went off to get their share.
Q. Did you form any opinion whether there was any foundation for these rumours?
A. I thought them very probable. I received a circumstantial story of a large party of villagers on the 12th and 13th about 3 miles from Amritsar and I thought it extremely likely that we should have some looting. (Evidence, Vol. III, page 6.)

Reports to the above effect were constantly coming to me, and the concerted attack on railway communications were further indications of the danger from outside. We found evidence afterwards that loot from the Banks had been taken out to the villages to demonstrate that the Raj had fallen and that the villages should rise and get their share.

There could be no reasonable doubt in my mind that any villagers in the meeting were there as sympathizers and adherents of the insurrection. I do not say that it was physically impossible for the crowd to have contained people who had not heard my own particular proclamation, and as I told the Committee there may conceivably have been many. I did not in fact believe there were, and I was, and am, convinced that substantially the whole crowd knew they were there in defiance of the authorities and in furtherance of the disorders.

The second point I wish to emphasize is the confirmation through the subsequent trials of offenders of my judgment, formed on the spot, that the meeting was engaged in listening to seditious harangues. Almost every speaker was a person who was afterwards convicted of sedition or had a warrant out against him. One was a man who is believed to have been the actual murderer of Mr. Scott. Is it possible, in view of this fact (which does not appear to have been before any of the authorities who have judged me), to doubt that my instinct and information were right, and that it was no innocent gathering, but a seditious and defiant mob?

10. EXPLANATION OF ORDER CLOSING THE STREET WHERE MISS SHERWOOD WAS ASSAULTED

The criticisms of my order issued on the 21st April prohibiting the use of the street where Miss Sherwood was attacked involves a matter quite separate from my action on the 13th in suppressing the revolt. It has been much misrepresented, and a short statement will, I hope, make clear its true nature. The order was only in force for a short time, and affected but a comparatively few people, and would not, I think, have been made so much of, but for the agitation against me for my suppression of the rising itself. It will be enough for me to explain my reasons and to submit that they were sufficient to exonerate me from any charge of military misconduct.

The attempted murder of Miss Sherwood was probably the most dastardly outrage in the whole rebellion. The fact that it was not murder was merely because her assailants made a mistake in thinking that they had completed their work. The door of a house in the street in question to which she fled after the first assault for protection, was slammed in her face, and after being again assaulted and beaten she was left for dead by the mob.

On the 21st April I closed this street during the daytime by putting a picket at each end, and ordered that no native should pass down it except on all fours. The order was not of course meant to be in any sense a permanent order, and the picket was only there for 12 hours in the daytime. It is a complete misunderstanding to suppose that I meant this order to be an insulting mark of race inferiority. The order meant that the street should be regarded as holy ground, and that, to mark this fact, no one was to traverse it except in a manner in which a place of special sanctity might naturally in the East be traversed. My object was not merely to impress the inhabitants, but to appeal to their moral sense in a way which I knew they would understand. It is a small point, but in fact "crawling order" is a misnomer; the order was to go on all fours in an attitude well understood by natives of India in relation to holy places.

I repeat what I said to the Committee that I had no conception that anybody would in fact use the street at all and, as is conceded by the Committee, hardly any people did so. A most trivial accident has been made use of to misrepresent my action. Immediately after placing the picquets on the street I had gone into the city with a party of British soldiers and had occasion while there to order the arrest of some men and send them back to the camp under escort. The non-commissioned officer with me and the British escort who took them back did not know the city and naturally went back by the way they came. When they arrived at the street the picquet strictly enforcing the order compelled the prisoners to go down it on all fours. I am of course responsible for this, but it was a pure accident and quite contrary to my intention.

It is very easy for a minor incident like this order, given in the circumstances in which it was given when the feelings of horror were strong upon everybody, to be misrepresented in quiet times by people at a great distance, and I am entitled to cite the judgment of the Adjutant-General of India five months after the event as a fair account of my motives and as containing an official view of my case which should exonerate me from censure for action taken according to the best of my judgment.

The Adjutant-General, after describing the attempted murder of Miss Sherwood and mentioning that an important political body had misrepresented it as being a "petty assault on a woman," proceeds as follows:—

"I feel sure that the Council will agree that it is
not surprising that the Officer in Command
took the view that some unusual measures were
necessary to bring home to the mob that such
acts of violence directed against defenceless
women could not be tolerated. Something was
required to strike the imagination and impress
on all the determination of the military
authorities to protect European women. This
Council can readily understand how easily the
feelings of soldiers would be outraged by acts of
this nature and that they might be led to
uncontrolled reprisals. Incidentally it is worthy
of note in this connection that we have no
charge against any of our soldiers during this
rebellion. It is easy, my Lord, to criticise the
orders issued by the officer in command at
Amritsar, but the circumstances were altogether
exceptional and the punishment, though
humiliating, was not such as to cause danger to
life or physical hurt. Except on one occasion
when a body of prisoners were brought down
the street in which Miss Sherwood had been
assaulted, no compulsion was brought to bear on
any individual to submit to the order. The order
remained in force for a period of five days and
there is good reason for the belief that, except
for the party of prisoners already mentioned,
those who were subjected to the order came
voluntarily to submit to it for the sake of
notoriety or martyrdom. One man after going

down the street on his hands and knees three times had to be stopped giving further exhibitions."

11. CHARGE OF UNDUE NEGLECT OF WOUNDED

Another subsidiary point of criticism is that I omitted to provide help for the wounded after the dispersal of the crowd. The Hunter Committee do not make this criticism. They appear to consider that, in view of the size of my force, I acted right in withdrawing at once to the Ram Bagh, and they say that it had not been proved to them that any wounded people were in fact exposed to unnecessary suffering from want of medical treatment. The Government of India in their Despatch do not blame me for this omission, but merely express regret that no action was taken either by the civil or military authorities to remove the dead or give aid to the wounded. But the Secretary of State is more severe and says:—

"that Brigadier-General Dyer should have taken no steps to see that some attempt was made to give medical assistance to the dying and wounded was an omission from his obvious duty."

I cannot help thinking that this criticism is really based on the misapprehension of fact to which I have already alluded, namely, that the casualties had occurred in a comparatively innocent gathering, and, as a whole, deserved the care of the authorities in the same way as would innocent sufferers in some big accident such as a flood or an earthquake during time otherwise peaceful. To succour any such innocent sufferers I should certainly have been prepared to make the utmost exertions and to take great risks. But in the actual circumstances of the case, I respectfully submit that the Hunter Committee were right to withhold adverse comment, and that it was not possible for me to use my small and hard-worked force for this purpose and that military consideration justified my action in withdrawing it at once to my headquarters. We had no field dressings with us. No medical officer could have lived in the city for an instant without a strong escort, and in my judgment none could be then spared. There is indeed no evidence to support the Secretary of State's apparent view that no assistance was given to the wounded by anyone. The hospitals were open and the Indian medical officers were there. Help from that quarter was available if asked for, and, as the Committee find, there was no evidence that unnecessary suffering had been caused to the wounded. I submit that there is no case whatever against me of any neglect of duty in regard to the wounded, and I venture to suggest that the criticism proceeds upon the assumption that the original firing was unnecessary and inhumane, the inference being that the failure to succour the innocent sufferers was equally inhumane.

I must add, in view of rumours which have come to my notice, that it is untrue that I issued orders that none of the wounded were to be attended to in hospital.

12. Summary of Military Considerations

Avoiding, so far as possible, repetition on what has already been narrated I summarize below the military situation as it appeared to me:—

(*a*.) The whole situation in Amritsar was primarily military. The civil authorities had already resigned power to Major Macdonald before I arrived.

(*b*.) The local tactical situation was hopeless unless a vigorous front was maintained and the initiative preserved throughout.

I had at the time about 407 British and 739 Indian troops, many of them only partially trained men in a city of 150,000 inflamed with criminal excesses and virtual immunity from authority, and a dense warlike population in the countryside ready to break into looting and disorder as soon as the news that the Raj had gone under went round.

The force was necessarily inadequate for anything but the bare protection of the civil lines, a few patrols, and guards at the nearest vital points. The railway as a whole, the city itself and the surrounding countryside had to be practically ignored so long as we remained on the defensive.

Had the city mob and the Manjha Sikhs joined hands, as assuredly they would soon have done, the troops and the civil lines would have been taken.

(*c*.) There were, among the Sikhs, some thousands of returned Ghadr revolutionaries and a vast number of demobilized soldiers; the latter would have been most formidable had their loyalty become affected in the general disappearance of Government authority.

(*d.*) The railway was vital. The Punjab has only one main railway line which passes over six large rivers. Communication with the North-West Frontier is entirely dependent on this line. Early in 1919, I made plans for the disposition of my troops in the event of a rising, and had taken special steps in order to keep the bridge-heads in my area clear.

There were many lesser bridges of military importance. It was impossible during the rising to find guards for all these vital points for want of troops. The report of the Committee provides ample material to show that the destruction of communications was carried out methodically and with concerted action.

(*e.*) I was alive to the situation on the frontier of Afghanistan. It is more than possible that the rising in Amritsar was precipitated by the action of the authorities in arresting the two chief agitators on the 10th. Had it been delayed four weeks it would have coincided with and paralysed the mobilization and concentration of the army for the work on the frontier.

(*f.*) I knew that attempts were being made to seduce my troops, and rumours came to me of similar attempts elsewhere.

(*g.*) The general military situation was grave. It is summarized in the passage from the evidence of Sir Michael O'Dwyer set out in the Committee's Report.

His is not a soldier's opinion, but it is plainly based on military reports and coincides with the information I had in April, 1919. The Army Council will be in possession of all the reports on these facts, and will no doubt refer to them for corroboration.

With the foregoing considerations before me and the daily reports and sights of Amritsar itself, I had no doubt that I was dealing with no mere local disturbance but a rebellion, which, whatever its origin, was aiming at something wide reaching and vastly more serious even than local riots and looting. The isolation of centres and the holding up of the movement of military reserves by destroying communications were essential features of the conspiracy.

I was conscious of a great offensive movement gathering against me, and knew that to sit still and await its complete mobilization would be fatal. When, therefore, the express challenge by this movement in the shape of the assembly in the Jallianwallah Bagh came to me, I knew that a military crisis had come, and that to view the assembly as a mere political gathering, requiring simply to be induced to go away because it was there in breach of an order, was wholly remote from the facts and the necessities of the case.

Amritsar was in fact the storm centre of a rebellion. The whole Punjab had its eyes on Amritsar, and the assembly of the crowd that afternoon was for all practical purposes a declaration of war by leaders whose hope and belief was that I should fail to take up the challenge.

13. Approval and Exoneration by Authorities

I must now direct attention to the way my case was treated by my superiors, both military and civil, from the date of the occurrence in April, 1919, till 22nd March, 1920, the first date when any official disapproval or censure was conveyed to me.

I submit that according to all military rule and precedent this treatment amounts to an exoneration which it is not now open to reverse.

The normal course of dealing with an officer whose conduct in an important matter is considered questionable, is, as is well known, to hold a Court of Enquiry and in the meantime to suspend him from his duties. No such action was taken in my case; and the following synopsis of events shows clearly the opposite nature of the course that was adopted:—

(*a*.) On 14th April, 1919, I reported the firing in the Bagh to Divisional Head-quarters in the Report B. 21.

(*b*.) On the next day, or the day following, my Divisional Commander, Major-General Beynon, conveyed to me his approval.

(*c*.) The Lieutenant-Governor about the same time agreed with the Divisional Commander.

(*d*.) On the 21st April, with the concurrence of the authorities, I went on a special mission to the Sikhs.

(*e*.) On 8th May, 1919, I was sent on active service in command of my Brigade to the frontier.

(*f.*) On about the 28th May, 1919, I was detailed to organize a force for the relief of Thal then invested by the Afghan Army. On this occasion I had an interview with General Sir Arthur Barrett, commanding at Peshawur. I had by then become aware that the influences which had inspired the rebellion were starting an agitation against those who had suppressed it.

Sir A. Barrett told me he wanted me to take command of the relief force. I told him that I wished, if possible, to be free from any anxiety about my action at Amritsar, which so far had been approved. He said: "That's all right, you would have heard about it long before this, if your action had not been approved." I give his precise words as nearly as I can.

(*g.*) About the end of July, 1919, I saw the Commander-in-Chief. He congratulated me on the relief of Thal. He said no word to me of censure about Amritsar, but merely ordered me to write a report on it, which I did. This report is dated the 25th August, 1919.

(*h.*) On 5th September, 1919, Major-General Beynon in his report on the rebellion made to Army Headquarters repeated his previous approval of my action, and added a testimony to my other services in connection with the rebellion: "The wisdom of General Dyer's action has been fully proved by the fact that there has been no further trouble at Amritsar" and later "The strong measures taken by General Dyer at

Amritsar had a far reaching effect, and prevented any further trouble in the Lahore Divisional Area. His knowledge of the Indian and his popularity with the Sikhs did much to restore confidence and loyalty in the surrounding districts."

(*i*.) On the 19th September, 1919, the Adjutant-General of India, who must clearly have had my report of 25th August, made a speech to the Legislative Council in which he reviewed the whole of my action. I annex a copy of the relevant part of his remarks as reported in the Official Report, as I regard his utterances, taken with what had already happened and in view of his position of Chief Staff Officer for disciplinary purposes in the Indian Army, as a complete exoneration of me and as conclusive against any further steps against me in the way of censure or penalty.

(*j*.) About October, 1919, I was promoted by being given permanent command of a Brigade.

(*k*.) On the 30th January, 1920, I was appointed to the temporary command of the Division, though owing to my illness which had been developing for some time, I never took up the appointment.

It was not till the 22nd March, 1920, that I was first told that my action at Amritsar was not approved, and that I was required to resign my appointment. This was at an interview with the Adjutant-General at Delhi, and the ground given was merely that the Hunter Committee had reported adversely to me. My evidence before the Committee was given on 19th November, 1919, and it will be appreciated from the above recital of events that it was not as a person on his defence that I came before it.

14. PROTEST AGAINST CHARGES OF INHUMANITY AND LOSS OF NERVE AND EVIDENCE OF CHARACTER

The Hunter Report acknowledges (and the Government of India and the Secretary of State concur) that I acted at Amritsar solely from a sense of duty and in the honest belief that I was carrying out my duty. A grave injustice is, however, done to me by the lack of any acknowledgment that I was possessed of any feelings of humanity or regard for human life. The lack of such acknowledgment, combined with the clear accusations made against me in the Minority Report of Prussian brutality and indifference to innocent suffering when in pursuit of military security has greatly prejudiced my case.

It is hardly possible that this prejudice would have arisen had I been accorded a proper warning of the case against me, and the usual facilities for defence, when evidence of my previous reputation and of surrounding circumstances could have been adduced to refute such calumnies. Some short allusion to these matters here is necessary in view of the neglect of them in the report.

My 34 years' service in India, during which I had reached the rank of Brigadier, and had received satisfactory reports throughout, should by itself be some testimony to my character in this regard.

Shortly prior to the events at Amritsar I had been called upon elsewhere in the neighbourhood on three separate occasions to deal with outbreaks and disturbances which were all in a sense forerunners of the rebellion. I referred to these occasions briefly in my official report to my military superior of the 26th August, 1919, and will not now repeat the details. While I claim no credit for my success in dealing with these minor crises after others had failed, I am entitled to insist that in the presence of mutiny and defiance of law I did not fire a single shot or use any violent or coercive method, I caused no loss of life, and I restored order by the arts of leadership and conciliation. It was from such recent successes and with such a record that I came to Amritsar on the night of 11th April.

During the 12th April I took no sort of offensive action against the city, though, as is conceded it was in a state of rebellion, hideous crimes had been perpetrated, and grave outbreaks were to be apprehended for the future. "Prussian methods" would have been easy; the city, in which admittedly Government rule had ceased and the mob was supreme, could have been bombed from aeroplanes (one was at my disposal) and bombarded by artillery, while offensive infantry action against the population could have been taken in detail with possibly advantageous results from a purely military standpoint. The Adjutant-General of India himself has referred to my policy of patience and conciliation on this day.

I claim no credit for an abstention which was my plain duty. But I am entitled to cite my conduct and record in such matters as some refutation of the charges of inhumanity levelled against me.

I can cite, for the same purpose, and indeed may be allowed to claim some credit for my pacification of the surrounding districts after the 21st April. The report itself makes plain the grave pre-occupation which the countryside and the Sikh population was to us during these critical days. I toured it with all the energy of which I was capable on the 21st April and succeeding days. I did not fire a shot or use any coercive measures against the population; I merely displayed my escort and used all the personal influence and diplomacy of which I was capable, getting hold of the leading men, appealing to them and reasoning with them, and thereby calming the spirit of unrest and insubordination that had been spreading from the city.

Of my personal success in this direction, I mention as proof, the fact that when, a fortnight or so later, the news of the Afghan attack filtered through to us, the leading men from the district came forward to me and offered me 10,000 Sikhs to fight for the Raj, and invited me to command them. I and my Brigade-Major received the unusual honour of being made Sikhs, and I was acclaimed on various occasions by native gatherings as the officer who had saved the situation. My Divisional Commander referred specially to the success of this mission in his despatch of the 5th September, 1919.

The Hunter Report would have provided more complete material for judging my conduct had it taken some express note of the foregoing matters.

The danger of injustice to me would have been still further diminished if some express reference had been made to what I told the Committee as to my own feelings about the firing on the crowd. I said then, and I say now, that the duty was a horrible duty, which I performed with dislike and distaste amounting to horror. I was sure of my duty as I approached the scene with my small body of troops; I was doubtful of my resolution to overcome my feelings and carry out my duty. The motives which inspired me I have already explained. I refer here to these matters of sentiment because the calumnies against my sense of humanity call for a reply in the absence of any protection afforded me by the Committee.

I am entitled further to ask that consideration should be given to all matters in my record which bear upon my character as a soldier, so far as they are relevant to this case.

My general record will be in possession of the War Office and I need not allude to it.

The incident of the relief of Thal will form a part of that record. I only mention the incident here because it occurred after the events at Amritsar, and helps to show that my faculties were alive and in good order and makes it unlikely that I am open to a charge of having lacked nerve or lost my head on the earlier occasion. For this purpose I include here the message I received from the Commander-in-Chief as showing that at that time my judgment and capacity were unimpaired:—

[Copy of a letter dated the 21st June, 1919, from the Brigadier-General General Staff, North-West Frontier Force, to the 16th Indian Division.]

"The following remarks by His Excellency, the Commander-in-Chief, with reference to the recent operations at Thal, are forwarded for communication to Brig.-General R.E.H.Dyer,C.B.:—
'The efforts made by Brig.-General Dyer from the time he arrived at Kohat were attended with full energy and competence. The manner in which he disposed of his troops, the full use he made of his artillery, the ardour he infused into his troops, denoted the hand of a Commander confident in his capacity and in his troops.

Brig.-General Dyer in this episode has given further evidence of power of Command.

Signed BRUCE HAY, *Lt.-Col., G.S.,*
for Brig.-General, General Staff,
N.W.F. Force.'"

It is necessary for me in this connection to say that it is untrue that I caused my party in the Jallianwallah Bagh to fire all its ammunition; I did not forget elementary musketry principles, and duly took care that a reserve of rounds was preserved sufficient for the extrication of the force, and subsequent emergencies. I do not follow the observation in the Secretary of State's despatch "until his ammunition supply was at the point of exhaustion."

The foregoing narrative and explanations sufficiently show that I neither lost my head, nor acted in any spirit of inhumanity.

Summary of Contentions and Conclusion

I have dealt in the foregoing paragraphs as briefly as possible with the mass of evidence and comment regarding my case. To attempt to cite all the relevant passages from the evidence and reports would obviously have been neither convenient nor practicable in a written statement, and I have confined myself to a few citations for the purpose of illustration only. If any points are considered not to have been sufficiently dealt with or any matters of doubt are found to arise as to which the Army Council desire further explanation, I request that Counsel may be heard orally on my behalf. I am advised that the whole case is one which can be more suitably dealt with by an oral argument, and as Counsel have already, in effect, been heard against me, it is only fair that I should not be condemned until I have had a similar advantage in making my defence. The Hunter Committee failed altogether to consider many points and much evidence which, had I been on my defence with properly formulated charges and expert assistance, would have been presented to it. Sir Michael O'Dwyer, who has more knowledge than anyone else of events in the Punjab has, he informs me, kindly offered to give the Army Council any information they may require, and I trust that, if necessary, they will avail themselves of this offer.

But I contend that I have said enough to show that upon the principal points of criticism I was justified in what I did, and that the circumstances required that I should act as I did.

In any case, I contend that I have abundantly shown, what alone it was necessary for me to show, that upon the facts before me and in the circumstances in which I was placed, I acted in good faith and had reasonable ground for my action.

I contend for these reasons that I should be finally exonerated from blame, and that all action of a penalizing character against me should be cancelled. As already stated I do not question the right of the Commander-in-Chief in India not to continue an officer in an appointment, if he considers that his employment therein is likely to prove an embarrassment to the authorities civil or military. But the exercise of such right need not involve censure or blame, and for censure or blame I submit there is in my case no ground.

The consistent course of official approval or exoneration to which I have called attention, and the irregularity so contrary to military law and so prejudicial to myself, with which my case was subsequently investigated are, I submit, obstacles prohibitive of all such censure or penalizing action.

My general record for restraint, discretion, and

decision during the rebellion and the actual services which I rendered in suppressing it in the most critical locality of the whole situation, and by my successful mission to the Sikhs should further be given proper weight.

The charges of inhumanity are, I submit, baseless, and I request that I may receive an explicit assurance that my character is regarded as completely from stain on this score.

Finally, I am confident that the Army Council in judging my conduct in an emergency, as critical as it was novel, will not fail to consider the responsibility which rested upon me and the possible consequences to the whole fabric of government in the Punjab, had I failed in energy and determination, and I claim to be entitled to the full countenance and support which was promised by the Government of India, when faced with the outbreak, to all officers engaged in the onerous duty of suppressing it.

I have the honour to be,
Sir,
Your obedient Servant,
R. E. H. DYER,
Brigadier-General, Indian Army.

Other titles in the series

John Profumo and Christine Keeler, 1963

"The story must start with Stephen Ward, aged fifty. The son of a clergyman, by profession he was an osteopath ... his skill was very considerable and he included among his patients many well-known people ... Yet at the same time he was utterly immoral."

The Backdrop

The beginning of the '60s saw the publication of 'Lady Chatterley's Lover' and the dawn of sexual and social liberation as traditional morals began to be questioned and in some instances swept away.

The Book

In spite of the recent spate of political falls from grace, the Profumo Affair remains the biggest scandal ever to hit British politics. The Minister of War was found to be having an affair with a call girl who had associations with a Russian naval officer at the height of the Cold War. There are questions of cover-up, lies told to Parliament, bribery and stories sold to the newspapers. Lord Denning's superbly written report into the scandal describes with astonishment and fascinated revulsion the extraordinary sexual behaviour of the ruling classes. Orgies, naked bathing, sado-masochistic gatherings of the great and good and ministers and judges cavorting in masks are all uncovered.

ISBN 0 11 702402 3   Price £6.99

The Loss of the Titanic, 1912

"From 'Mesabe' to 'Titanic' and all east bound ships. Ice report in Latitude 42N to 41.25N; Longitude 49 to 50.30W. Saw much Heavy Pack Ice and a great number of Large Icebergs. Also Field Ice. Weather good. Clear."

The Backdrop

The watchwords were "bigger, better, faster, more luxurious" as builders of ocean-going vessels strove to outdo each other in their race to capitalise on a new golden age of travel.

The Book

The story of the sinking of the *Titanic*, as told by the official enquiry, reveals some remarkable facts which have been lost in popular re-tellings of the story. A ship of the same line, only a few miles away from the *Titanic* as she sank, should have been able to rescue passengers, so why did this not happen? Readers of this fascinating report will discover that many such questions remain unanswered and that the full story of a tragedy which has entered into popular mythology has by no means been told.

ISBN 0 11 702403 1   Price £6.99

Tragedy at Bethnal Green: 1943

"Immediately the alert was sounded a large number of people left their houses in the utmost haste for shelter. A great many were running. Two cinemas at least in the near vicinity disgorged a large number of people and at least three omnibuses set down their passengers outside the shelter."

The Backdrop

The beleaguered East End of London had borne much of the brunt of the Blitz but, in 1943, four years into WWII, it seemed that the worst of the bombing was over.

The Book

The new unfinished tube station at Bethnal Green was one of the largest air raid shelters in London. After a warning siren sounded on 3 March 1943, there was a rush to the shelter. By 8.20pm, a matter of minutes after the alarm had sounded, 174 people lay dead, crushed in their attempt to get into the tube station's booking hall. At the official enquiry, questions were asked about the behaviour of certain officials and whether the accident could have been prevented.

ISBN 0 11 702404 X   Price £6.99

The Judgement of Nuremberg, 1946

"Efficient and enduring intimidation can only be achieved either by Capital Punishment or by measures by which the relatives of the criminal and the population do not know the fate of the criminal. This aim is achieved when the criminal is transferred to Germany."

The Backdrop

WWII is over, there is a climate of jubilation and optimism as the Allies look to rebuilding Europe for the future but the perpetrators of Nazi War crimes have still to be reckoned with, and the full extent of their atrocities is as yet widely unknown.

The Book

Today, we have lived with the full knowledge of the extent of Nazi atrocities for over half a century and yet they still retain their power to shock. Imagine what it was like as they were being revealed in the full extent of their horror for the first time. In this book the judges at the Nuremberg Trials take it in turn to describe the indictments handed down to the defendants and their crimes. The entire history, purpose and method of the Nazi party since its foundation in 1918 is revealed and described in chilling detail.

ISBN 0 11 702406 6   Price £6.99

The Boer War 1900: Ladysmith and Mafeking

"4th February – From General Sir Redvers Buller to Field-Marshal Lord Roberts … I have today received your letter of 26 January. White keeps a stiff upper lip, but some of those under him are desponding. He calculates he has now 7000 effectives. They are eating their horses and have very little else. He expects to be attacked in force this week … "

The Backdrop

The Boer War is often regarded as one of the first truly modern wars, as the British Army, using traditional tactics, came close to being defeated by a Boer force which deployed what was almost a guerrilla strategy in punishing terrain.

The Book

Within weeks of the outbreak of fighting in South Africa, two sections of the British Army were besieged at Ladysmith and Mafeking. Beginning with despatches describing the losses suffered by the British Army at Spion Kop on its way to rescue the garrison at Ladysmith, the book goes on to describe the lifting of the siege. The second part of the book gives Lord Baden Powell's account of the siege of Mafeking and how the soldiers and civilians coped with the inevitable hardship.

ISBN 0 11 702408 2   Price £6.99

The British Invasion of Tibet:
Colonel Younghusband, 1904

"On the 13th January I paid ceremonial visit to the Tibetans at Guru, six miles further down the valley in order that by informal discussion I might assure myself of their real attitude. There were present at the interview three monks and one general from Lhasa. These monks were low-bred persons, insolent, rude and intensely hostile; the generals, on the other hand, were polite and well-bred."

The Backdrop

At the turn of the century, the British Empire was at its height, with its army at the forefront of the mission to bring what the Empire saw as the tremendous civilising benefits of the British way of life to those nations which it regarded as still languishing in the dark ages.

The Book

In 1901, a British missionary force under the leadership of Colonel Francis Younghusband crossed over the border from British India and invaded Tibet. Younghusband insisted on the presence of the Dalai Lama at meetings to give tribute to the British and their Empire. The Dalai Lama merely replied that he must withdraw. Unable to tolerate such an insolent attitude, Younghusband marched forward and inflicted considerable defeats on the Tibetans in several one-sided battles.

ISBN 0 11 702409 0   Price £6.99

War 1914:Punishing the Serbs

" ... *I said that this would make it easier for others such as Russia to counsel moderation in Belgrade. In fact, the more Austria could keep her demand within reasonable limits, and the stronger the justification she could produce for making any demands, the more chance there would be for smoothing things over. I hated the idea of a war between any of the Great Powers, and that any of them should be dragged into a war by Serbia would be detestable.*"

The Backdrop
In Europe before WWI, diplomacy between the Embassies was practised with a considered restraint and politeness which provided an ironic contrast to the momentous events transforming Europe forever.

The Book
Dealing with the fortnight leading up to the outbreak of the First World War, the book mirrors recent events in Serbia to an astonishing extent. Some argued for immediate and decisive military action to punish Serbia for the murder of the Archduke Franz Ferdinand. Others pleaded that a war should not be fought over Serbia. The powers involved are by turn angry, conciliatory and, finally, warlike. Events take their course as the great war machine grinds into action.

ISBN 0 11 702410 4   Price £6.99

War 1939: Dealing with Adolf Hitler

"Herr Hitler asserted that 'I did not care how many Germans were being slaughtered in Poland'. This gratuitous impugnment of the humanity of His Majesty's Government and of myself provoked a heated retort on my part and the remainder of the interview was of a somewhat strong character."

The Backdrop

As he presided over the rebuilding of a Germany shattered and humiliated after WWI, opinion regarding Hitler and his intentions was divided and the question of whether his ultimate aim was military domination by no means certain.

The Book

Sir Nevile Henderson, the British ambassador in Berlin in 1939, describes here, in his report to Parliament, the failure of his mission and the events leading up to the outbreak of war. He tells of his attempts to deal with both Hitler and von Ribbentrop to maintain peace and gives an account of the changes in German foreign policy regarding Poland.

ISBN 0 11 702411 2   Price £6.99

The Strange Story of Adolph Beck

"He said he was Lord Winton de Willoughby. He asked why I lived alone in a flat. I said I had an income and wished to do so … Two or three hours after he had gone I missed some tigers' claws and the teeth of an animal mounted in silver with my monogram."

The Backdrop
The foggy streets of Edwardian London were alive with cads, swindlers, ladies of dubious reputation and all manner of low life who fed on human frailty.

The Book
In 1895, Adolph Beck was arrested and convicted of the crimes of deception and larceny. Using the alias Lord Winton de Willoughby, he had entered into the apartments of several ladies, some of whom preferred, for obvious reasons, not to give their names. The ladies gave evidence, as did a handwriting expert, and Mr Beck was imprisoned. But an utterly bizarre sequence of events culminated in a judge who declared that, since he could himself determine perfectly whether the accused was of the criminal classes or not, juries should never be allowed to decide the outcome of a trial. The account given here is of one of the strangest true stories in the entire British legal history.

ISBN 0 11 702414 7   Price £6.99

Rillington Place

" 'I want to give myself up. I have disposed of my wife.' 'What do you mean?' said the Constable. Evans replied, 'I put her down the drain.' The officer told Evans to think again before he said any more, and Evans said, 'I know what I am saying. I cannot sleep and I want to get it off my chest.' "

The Backdrop

The serial killer, or mass-murderer, is often seen as a creation of modern society. Quiet killers, however, drawing no attention to themselves in the teeming streets of the metropolis, have been responsible for some of the most notorious crimes of the 20th century.

The Book

In 1950, Timothy Evans was hanged for the self-confessed murder of his wife and daughter at 10 Rillington Place, Notting Hill but their bodies could not be found. Two years later, a couple moved into the same ground floor flat, vacated by a man named Christie. They discovered bodies in cupboards, Christie's wife under the floorboards and Evans's wife and daughter in the garden shed. Christie was convicted of mass murder and hanged. At two subsequent enquiries, it was suggested that Evans may not have been a murderer. If not, why did he confess?

ISBN 0 11 702417 1   Price £6.99

Wilfrid Blunt's Egyptian Garden: Fox Hunting in Cairo

"Cairo. July 23, 1901 – On Sunday morning a fox-hunt was taking place near Cairo, in the desert, the hounds following a scent crossed the boundary-wall of Mr. Wilfrid Blunt's property, and two of the field, being British officers, who were acting as whips, went in to turn them back. Mr. Blunt's watchmen surrounded them, and, although they explained their intention, treated them with considerable violence."

The Backdrop

In the days of Empire, the British way of life was carried on with a blithe disregard for local peculiarities and this went hand in hand with a sometimes benevolent, sometimes despotic, belief in the innate inferiority of those under its thumb.

The Book

In 1900, the Imperial British Army occupied Egypt and, in order to provide sport for the officers who were kicking their heels, a pack of hounds was shipped out from England to hunt the Egyptian fox. Unfortunately, the desert provides poor cover and, one day, the pack, followed in hot pursuit by the officers, found itself in the garden of the rich and eccentric poet Wilfrid Scarwen Blunt. Attempting to protect the absent Mr. Blunt's property, his servants tried to prevent the hunt and were promptly arrested. Mr. Blunt objected to the officers' behaviour, both to the government and the press, and the matter became quite a scandal.

ISBN 0 11 702416 3   Price £6.99

R.101: the Airship Disaster, 1930

" … about seven and a half hours later, shortly after two o'clock in the morning of October 5th, she came to earth two hundred and sixteen miles away in undulating country south of the town of Beauvais in France, and immediately became a blazing wreck. Of the fifty-four people on board, all but eight perished instantly in the flames … "

The Backdrop

In the golden age of air travel, the R.101 was the biggest and most splendid airship in the world. On the evening of the 4th October 1930 she left her mooring mast at Cardington on her ill-fated journey to India. As the ship ploughed on through increasingly threatening weather, the Air Minister and his guests retired to their well appointed cabins. Seven hours later, her burning frame lay shattered on a hillside in France.

The Book

As the shocked nation mourned, a Court of Inquiry was set up to investigate the disaster. Its report exposed the public pressure exerted by the Air Minister, Lord Thomson, whose enthusiastic backing for the project brought forward the date for its inaugural flight without proper trials. Whatever the mechanical causes of the crash, it is clear that designers, constructors and crew alike had been unduly hurried at the last minute. The early end of the airship in modern commercial flight was the result.

ISBN 0 11 702407 4   Price £6.99